The Blac
Interviews with N

Never-before published interviews with those at the heart of Goebbels' propaganda machine—the Nazi 'Marilyn Monroe', Lili Marlene's composer, Leni Riefenstahl's cameraman, Goebbels' secretary and many more.

KAREN LIEBREICH is an author, historian, gardener and film-maker. She has a doctorate in history from Cambridge University, and worked for the BBC making TV documentaries on European silent cinema and Nazi film. She has written several non-fiction books. She was awarded an MBE in 2013.

"If the Nazis were movie mad, then the Third Reich was movie made." Eric Rentschler, author of *The Ministry of Illusion: Nazi Cinema and Its Afterlife*

ALSO BY KAREN LIEBREICH

*Fallen Order: Intrigue, Heresy and Scandal
in the Rome of Galileo and Caravaggio*

The Letter in the Bottle

The Family Kitchen Garden

For children

UneXplained: Spine-tingling Tales

The Black Page
Interviews with Nazi Film-makers

Karen Liebreich

Published as an e-book in 2017 by McHugh Publications.
Paperback edition published in Great Britain
in 2017 by McHugh Publications

Copyright © Karen Liebreich, 2017

The moral right of Karen Liebreich to be identified as the
author of this work has been asserted by her in accordance
with the Copyright, Designs and Patents Act of 1988.

All rights reserved. No part of this publication may be
reproduced, stored in a retrieval system, or transmitted in any
form or by any means, electronic, mechanical, photocopying,
recording, or otherwise, without the prior permission of both
the copyright owner and the above author of this book.

Every effort has been made to trace all copyright holders.
The author will be pleased to make good any omissions or
rectify any mistakes brought to their attention at the earliest
opportunity.

978-0-9569164-3-3

www.karenliebreich.com

Contents

Introduction 7

Wilfred von Oven 19
Press Officer to Goebbels

Marianne Hoppe 32
Actress

Gerhard Huttula 39
Cameraman, special effects

Rudolf Klicks 48
Child actor, film editor

Erich Kästner 50
Camera inventor

Brigitte Mira: Actress 53
Margot Hielscher: Actress, singer

Theodor Nischwitz: 57
Special Effects Cinematographer
Lida Baarova, actress, lover of Goebbels

Fritz Hippler 65
Director, Reich's Film Department

Brunhilde Pomsel 68
Secretary to Joseph Goebbels

Hans-Otto Meissner 75
Diplomat

Hans Feld: Film critic 80
Leni Riefenstahl: Actress, director

Walter Frentz 87
Cameraman

Arthur Maria Rabenalt 91
Director

Norbert Schultze 93
Composer

Kristina Söderbaum 102
Actress

Conclusion 119
List of films mentioned 120
Filmography of interviewees 131
Bibliography 138

Introduction

In the early 1990s, I interviewed many people associated with the world of film under the Nazis. I spoke to actors and actresses, film directors, editors, composers, cameramen, critics and journalists, camera inventors, press officers, diplomats and politicians. My aim was to judge their suitability for appearing in a BBC television programme about propaganda, but our conversations covered many aspects of their work in the 1930s and 40s. Later, we selected some of them for official interviews, but many did not make the final cut. Even of those we interviewed, the BBC used only a few lines of what they said. This book is based on those interviews, never published before, with people whose work lay at the very centre of the Nazi regime. Many had never spoken of their experience on the record before, nor have they since.

Propaganda was of crucial importance for Hitler and Goebbels, and film was one of its most effective weapons. In *Mein Kampf*, first published in 1925, Hitler devotes several chapters to the importance of propaganda, emphasising imagery over the printed word: "The mass of the people as such is lazy. The picture in all its forms up to the film has greater possibilities. Here a man needs to use his brains even less. It suffices to look... and thus many will more readily accept a pictorial presentation than read an article of any length. The picture brings them in a much briefer time, I might almost say at one stroke, the enlightenment which they obtain from written matter only after arduous reading."[1]

The earliest Nazi films were essentially documentaries about party rallies. With the establishment of a film office in 1931, production began on a series of unsubtle documentaries, such as *Hitler's Kampf um Deutschland (Hitler's Fight for Germany)* and *Das junge Deutschland marschiert (German Youth on the March)*. Once Joseph Goebbels was put in charge of film policy, a broader range of film was embraced, where the dramatic element would include escapist, morale-boosting entertainment often with a strong, almost subconscious message. Nevertheless, more blunt propaganda films, such as *Hitlerjunge Quex Hitler Youth Quex)* or *Triumph des Willens (Triumph of the Will)* still continued to appear. Much later, in 1942, Goebbels decreed that the ideal film would be about 80 percent light entertainment, 20 percent propaganda.

"We are convinced that in general film is one of the most modern and far-reaching methods of influencing the masses. A regime thus must not allow film to go its

---

[1] Adolf Hitler, *Mein Kampf*, pp.470-471.
https://ia800302.us.archive.org/16/items/Mein_Kampf_Facsimilie/MK.pdf

own way" said Goebbels in a speech he gave in 1934[2], not long after becoming minister in charge of propaganda. Whether it was the weekly newsreels that provided carefully tailored news and information, the fluffy comedies and heart-warming romances that distracted people from the grim realities of everyday life, the role-playing historical dramas, or the more targeted films that were used to prepare the way for new policies and to underline important aspects of the regime's progress, every film formed part of a general strategy overseen by the Reich's Ministry of Public Enlightenment and Propaganda, with the Minister himself closely involved at all levels. Between 1933 and 1945 there were 1,086 premieres of German feature films, a staggering one or two a week.[3] Whether or not the cinema was as effective as he hoped has been a matter of much academic discussion over the years.

* * *

I started work on this project in early 1991, reading widely, watching videos of old films, telephoning around and trying to establish some kind of rapport with the elderly

---

[2] Speech of 9 February 1934, cited in David Weinberg, "Approaches to the Study of Film in the Third Reich: A Critical Appraisal," *Journal of Contemporary History*, vol.19, no.1 (Jan 1984) pp.105-126, p.105.

[3] Lutz Koepnick, *The Dark Mirror: German Cinema Between Hitler and Hollywood* (Berkeley: University of California Press, 2002), p.24.

Nazis I managed to find. The selection of interviewees was, of necessity, unscientific. It was more than forty-five years since the end of the Second World War, and many of the protagonists were already long dead. The sole advantage I had over earlier researchers was that those who were still alive had nothing to lose professionally or personally by speaking freely. Most had been able to resume their post-war careers, occasionally after a hiatus for judicial investigation or a spell in a Russian labour camp, but all were retired and generally living in comfortable circumstances. For some, talking to me was a chance to set the record straight or simply to recall the good old days. So the rather arbitrary selection of interviewees consisted of those people that I managed to track down and convince to be interviewed who had worked in the German film industry during the Nazi period, whether as actors, directors, technicians, or film critics – and who were still alive and had something interesting to tell.

By September 1991, I was ready to fly out to Germany and Switzerland for a recce. I took copious notes to relay my findings to the producer and to inform our choice of interviewees, and it is these notes that form the basis of much of what follows. The aim of the notes was to discover whether the participant would make an interesting interviewee, not initially to extract an in-depth or comprehensive analysis of the techniques of creating successful propaganda films.

The notes reflect the constraints of research in that era, a time before the Internet, when watching a film clip usually involved a trip to the National Film Archive in Koblenz and a great deal of time-consuming threading, spooling and unspooling of films on clunky viewing tables. I was lucky enough to find a knowledgeable German journalist and film buff, Werner Rulf, whose kitchen cupboards at home in West London were crammed with DVDs of German comedies and dramas from the 1930s and '40s. While editing my notes, I have now been able, at the click of a cursor, to check out various films and fellow-actors that my interviewees mentioned; it is possible at last to make sense of some of the throwaway comments they made to me at the time.

How short-sighted it now seems that, having picked out the few phrases and clips we needed to cut into our film, the BBC discarded the rest of the interviews. According to their archives, they retained neither rushes nor transcripts. These notes are almost certainly all that remains. The interviews were used in *We have ways of making you think*, a three-part series on propaganda in various countries that Laurence Rees produced and directed. Later, the BBC repeated our film as an hour-long episode for *Timewatch*, a long-running documentary series that ran on BBC2 from 1982 to 2006. Rees became fascinated by the Nazis, and after this programme would go on to direct several award-winning series on the subject, most notably *The Nazis: A Warning from History*, along with several accompanying books.

With some blurring at the edges, the interviewees fall into a few discrete categories. Of course, it is easy to make judgements from a post-Holocaust perspective, but nevertheless there were those, such as Wilfred von Oven, Fritz Hippler and Hans-Otto Meissner, whom one could fairly describe as unregenerate Nazis. Certainly for von Oven, the period he spent working as press attaché to Joseph Goebbels was the best time of his life. A young and handsome lieutenant, he was seconded to one of the men at the very centre of power, and life was great fun. None of these three interviewees showed any regrets, apart from being on the losing side, and perhaps—though less important in the great scheme of things—not finishing off the job with regard to the Jews. Meissner and Hippler were living in some luxury when we interviewed them, Meissner in his spacious hunting lodge outside Munich, Hippler on his terrace overlooking Hitler's Eagle's Nest at Berchtesgaden in the Bavarian Alps. Von Oven flew in from Argentina on one of his regular book publicity cum neo-Nazi political tours.

We also interviewed those who seemed to have shed their beliefs after the war, but who were enthusiastic at the time. These included film director Arthur Maria Rabenalt, who specialised in musicals, circus and animal films, and who had a surprise hit with a patriotic riding film. Walter Frentz joined the SS in 1941 and became Hitler's personal cameraman, after working with Riefenstahl on both of her big Nazi-era films. We spoke with Margot Hielscher, a beautiful actress who rivals said slept her way to some good roles via Goebbels' casting couch.

Then there were some amiable fellow travellers, who had never really thought through what they might have done for the regime and seemed unaware that it had even involved them in any way. This category included cameraman Gerhard Huttula, who created an iconic scene, perhaps one of the most famous in the history of German cinema, in which Baron Münchhausen hitches a ride on a cannon ball. It also included Goebbels' little secretary, Brunhilde Pomsel, and the great film star Kristina Söderbaum, the Marilyn Monroe of the Nazi era, who portrayed injured Aryan womanhood so many times in some of the most celebrated films of the era.

Only one or two of our interviewees showed any sign of self-awareness or self-doubt about their contribution to the success of the regime. Marianne Hoppe, a famous leading actress, seemed to regret her complicity, but perhaps mainly for the shadow it cast on her reputation. Norbert Schultze, composer of Lili Marlene and many other wartime hits, was faintly surprised at writing songs such as *Bomben auf Engelland*

(Bombs on England) but he admitted without hesitation that he would do it all over again to help his Fatherland.

Such regrets as our interviewees voiced were usually limited to the damage their work may have done to their own post-war careers. For most, it had been a job, often a good and interesting one, maybe even a vocation. Keeping the home fires burning, helping boost morale, supporting our troops at the front – these are still considered legitimate, even praiseworthy, aims. Co-opting art and entertainment to promote genocide is another matter. In this defining period of the twentieth century, an era that saw the first Agfacolor film, there were many shades of grey.

* * *

Joseph Goebbels is the central personality in any discussion of film during the Nazi period. Born in 1897 of humble Catholic origins, Goebbels had a sickly childhood that left him with a club foot and a permanent limp. He did well at school and went on to complete a doctorate in German literary history. In a direct echo of his leader's failed attempts to make his mark as an artist, Goebbels' efforts at novel and play-writing were also unsuccessful, and he began to turn his attention towards National Socialist politics. Almost immediately he was swept away by Hitler's charisma: "Hitler is an idealistic enthusiast. A man who will bring new belief to the Germans. I'm reading his speech, letting myself be carried away by him and up to the stars."[4] From 1924 onwards, Goebbels was Hitler's devoted follower, even unto death. In August 1926 he became Gauleiter for the Berlin sector, and in 1930 was put in charge of all Nazi newspapers and propaganda. The following year, with Hitler's blessing, he married the wealthy divorcee Magda Quandt who would serve as a public role model for Nazi womanhood: beautiful, blonde, and fertile.

Disappointed not to be appointed Minister for Culture when Hitler became Chancellor on 30 January 1933, Goebbels was rewarded shortly after the Reichstag Fire of 27 February 1933 with the position of head of the Reich's Ministry of Public Enlightenment and Propaganda. Huge party rallies, book burnings, and purges of non-Aryans swiftly followed.

On 28 March 1933, just two weeks after the establishment of the new Propaganda Ministry, Goebbels called a meeting of DACHO, the Association of German Film Producers, at the Hotel Kaiserhof in Berlin, where he explained in detail to the assembled members of the industry just how their films were sabotaging the work of the Führer. From now on, he declared, Jews would not be permitted to work in the industry. Hans Feld, one of our

---

[4] Quoted in Peter Longerich, *Goebbels: A Biography* (London: Bodley Head, 2015).

interviewees, was present and described the meeting. The Reich's Film Chamber (Reichsfilmkammer) was created in June 1933, three months after Goebbels became Minister. Anyone wishing to pursue a career in film was required to be a member, and anyone unable to prove his Aryan descent was thus automatically excluded. The Chamber controlled everything, from cinema ticket prices to mandatory showing of newsreels. A Reichsfilmdramaturg was appointed in 1934, whose job was to pre-censor and accredit all scripts, to supplement the Film Censor who would only deal with completed films. The Dramaturg would judge whether "the film could either endanger the vital interests of the state or the public order or security, or endanger National Socialist, religious, moral or artistic sentiment."[5]

In April 1934 the Hitler Youth organization in Cologne organised a Youth Film Hour (Jugendfilmstunde), focussing on films considered specially relevant to the development – or to put it more bluntly, indoctrination – of young people, and this soon became mandatory for all Hitler-Jugend groups. Within two years 70,000 schools had been supplied with 16mm projectors[6]. In 1936, the regime abolished film criticism,

---

[5] Paragraph 7 of the Cinematic Act, February 16, 1934, quoted in Christelle Georgette Le Faucheur, *Defining Nazi Film: The Film Press and the German Cinematic Project, 1933-1945* (Austin: PhD dissertation, University of Texas, 2012), p.12.

[6] David Stewart Hull, *Film in the Third Reich: A study of the German Cinema, 1933-45* (University of California Press, 1969), p.51.

replacing it with "Filmbeobachtung", film observations. Goebbels was now the ultimate judge of what was to be put before the German public's eyes. A few years later, a film school, the Deutsche Filmakademie Babelsberg, was added to the portfolio, and the nationalisation of all the film production companies by November 1942[7] completed the party's monopoly over the film industry.

The Minister took a personal interest in all the projects of the film industry, partly as a self-proclaimed film buff, partly because films were seen as such a key weapon in the propaganda armoury, second only to radio. Mass rallies, newsprint, posters, music, and theatre all played their part, but film was the prime entertainment medium of the masses and was, along with the accompanying newsreels that usually preceded the main feature, of paramount importance. For remote areas, the Propaganda Ministry even deployed 300 film trucks and two trains to bring film to village inns and halls.[8] As Goebbels explained, "War cannot be won without optimism; it is as important as cannons and weapons…. The darker our streets are, the brighter our theatres and film cinemas must be."[9]

---

[7] Le Faucheur, *op. cit.,* p.13.
[8] Michael Munn, *Hitler and the Nazi Cult of Celebrity* (London: Robson Press, 2012).
[9] http://research.calvin.edu/german-propaganda-archive/images/ws/sachsen-82-1939.jpg, 17 November 1939 and Guido Knopp, *Hitler's Women* (New York: Routledge, 2001), p.229.

Goebbels' ambitions were infinite. "It is my ultimate goal to establish the German film as the dominant cultural world power," he wrote in 1941.[10] He may not have succeeded, but it was not for want of trying, and the attempt remains unprecedented to this day. As film-maker Volker Schloendorff noted, "Goebbels is more fascinating today than Hitler – at least to media people. No-one has ever had such exclusive power over all the media in existence at the time and never has someone in a position of responsibility pursued his task with such passion as that of a frustrated artist."

* * *

Initially I flew alone to Berlin on 30 September 1991 for a preliminary round of interviews and research; later I returned with producer Laurence Rees and the film crew. I had set up several locations, including the Babelsberg film studios, a couple of villas near the Wannsee with links to Joseph Goebbels—Schwanenwerder and Krummelanke—and the old cinema in Oranienburg. I had also arranged interviews with a series of elderly Germans. From Berlin I went on to Munich and Switzerland, via Lake Constance for more interviews, often in the interviewees' own houses. The notes that follow are the result.

---

[10] Cited in Felix Moeller, *The Film Minister: Goebbels and the Cinema in the Third Reich* (Stuttgart/London: Edition Alex Menges, 2000), p.8, reviewed by Jonathan Dawson in *Senses of Cinema*, July 2002.

Wilfred von Oven

Our first filmed interview was with Wilfred von Oven, who had been Goebbels' personal press officer (*Pressereferent*) from May 1943 to 22 April 1945, a week before the final defeat of the Nazi regime. In a later interview with an American journalist he described his early years. He was born in Bolivia, where his father was working as a banker, but the family soon returned to Europe, and his father was killed in the First World War at Flanders. "My family lived at that time in Silesia," he said. "Hundreds and hundreds of Jews arrived from the east, with their strange and dirty and poor clothes. They got on trains, went to Berlin and, in a few years—well, they were obviously better at managing money than the Germans. And they gained very important positions. And a very negative atmosphere grew among the two races. I know this very well because at that time I was 15 or 16 years old. And that is the fighting age, when you are ready to do anything."[11] Von Oven went into journalism and first saw combat in the late 1930s with the Condor Legion, a German force that supported Franco during the Spanish Civil War. He became a war reporter with the supreme command of the German Army during the invasions of Poland, France, the Balkans and Russia. Then he got his

---

[11] Interview by Sebastian Rotella for *Los Angeles Times*, 17 March 2000, http://articles.latimes.com/2000/mar/17/news/mn-9874/2

dream job, working directly for the Minister of Propaganda.

After the war he fled to Argentina, where he founded a German language newspaper for the local (Nazi) expats, which reached a circulation of some 30,000, one of the largest of any German publication outside Europe, and adapted his diaries into a book titled *Finale Furioso: Mit Goebbels bis zum Ende (With Goebbels to the Bitter End)*. Originally published in 1949, it was re-published in 1974 by Gerhard Frey's company. Frey was the founder of the Deutsche Volksunion, a nationalist anti-immigration political party that he had set up in 1971, and between his publishing empire and his politics, he sat at the very centre of Germany's post-war extreme right. Von Oven was a regular contributor to his newspapers as well as editor of *Deutschland in Geschichte und Gegenwart (Germany Past and Present)*, an "extremist, right-wing quarterly journal."[12] A few years after our interview, in 1997, von Oven would be awarded the annual Ulrich von Hutten medal by the Society for Free Journalism (Gesellschaft für freie Publizistik), an association that former Nazi Party and SS members set up to present what they see as the correct version of the origins of the Second World War and to combat the distortions of current historic portrayals of National Socialism.

---

[12] Note from *Defense Documents of Irving vs Lipstadt Trial*, www.hdot.org/en/trial/defense/evans/530cii.html

I tracked down von Oven initially via his publisher, and then through a network of old and new Nazis, as he was due to visit Germany to give a lecture tour to the faithful. This network yielded several addresses of other old Nazis who were available to lecture—those with fond memories of the good old days—and also an up-and-coming generation of neo-Nazis.

I found a good place to interview von Oven, and it was hearing about the venue that decided him in favour of the meeting. As Gauleiter of Mark Brandenburg, Goebbels wanted a mansion that had the true "Brandenburg atmosphere." For his thirty-ninth birthday, in October 1936, the town of Berlin gave him a lodge (a *"Blockhaus"*) called Lanke on the Bogensee, some forty kilometres north of Berlin. Goebbels was delighted. In his diary he wrote, "I am so excited... the house is wonderful. A jewel-box. Here it is possible to rest and work. What an idyll. So romantic and peaceful. I am completely happy."[13]

Lanke became for him his "little Paradise", where he could read and write in peace. Within four days of receiving his "gift" from the city, he wrote in his diary on 3 November 1936, "Completely alone. I am so happy. It is completely still and quiet here. I work, read, write and am happy. All around me forest, withered foliage, fog, rain.

---

[13] Stefan Berkholz, *Goebbels' Waldhof am Bogensee. Vom Liebesnest zur DDR-Propagandastätte* (Berlin: Christoph Links Verlag, 2004). Goebbels' Diary, quoted on p.11. Author's translations.

An idyll of solitude." Two days later, still in his forest paradise, Goebbels noted in his diary, "This Jewish plague must be rooted out. Completely and utterly. Nothing must be left of it."[14] Lanke was a source of inspiration for him.

Over the following few years, Goebbels had the building rebuilt at great expense, with thirty bedrooms, forty service rooms, sixty telephones and so on, despite some concerns from his neighbours—namely Hermann Göring, who along with all his other titles was the Reichsjägermeister (the Reich's Chief Hunter) and in charge of the Reich's forests, and whose country house lay only a few kilometres away. Lanke was to become a long, low building, its two wings stretching around a central open courtyard at the front. It had a gabled entrance, white walls, and a pointed roof, in a sort of pseudo rancho style. A dense forest surrounded the house, and the back of the building faced directly onto a terrace of yellow, green, and blue tiles, backed by an amazing wall of dark green trees, like something out of an ominous Grimm's fairytale. Six tall windows created a glass wall for the entire sitting room, which seemed to have a forest mural along one side; at the press of a button the glass split in two, with the top half rising into the ceiling and the bottom dropping down below the floorboards. This was undoubtedly the highlight of the house. Goebbels, as head of the Nazi film industry, had ordered the top scene

---

[14] Berkholz, *Goebbels' Waldhof*, p.14.

designers to create these 'film technique windows' for his personal gratification. In our interview, von Oven said: "This terrace was ideal for enjoying nature. I can imagine that one could have held wonderful dances here. The background of the Brandenburg countryside is quite something, it was all around us—the total silence and the peace of life in the countryside. We often sat inside. Then Goebbels would do one of his tricks: to the astonishment of all the guests—I saw it then, just imagine, all those years ago, I saw it—he would lower them [the windows] again!" The costs of the rebuilding and running of Lanke spiralled to almost 3 million Reichsmark, and Goebbels became concerned, until it was conveniently decided that the film industry, based at nearby Babelsberg Studios, and the town of Berlin, would pay for everything.[15]

After the war, the house became part of a high school for communist cadres of the Socialist party. The famed private cinema was reduced to a little supermarket, and when I visited it was locked up and full of junk; no-one could find the keys. After the fall of the Berlin Wall, Lanke briefly became a training centre. The main room and the forest terrace served as an upmarket restaurant for state employees; the ceilings, wall decorations, mechanical sliding windows, and floors were all original, though the original lake had receded back out of sight. The waiters still wore black tuxedos, and the table linen in the

---

[15] Berkholz, *Goebbels' Waldhof*, p.45.

restaurant was starched white. But with the fall of the Wall it needed a new role. When I approached them to ask about filming, the estate was delighted. There were plans to turn the house into a luxury hotel, and the publicity from a BBC film was just the fillip they felt they needed. They offered us rooms at Lanke while we filmed, and suggested that we could even sleep in Goebbels' old bedroom. Laurence Rees jumped at the suggestion. I could imagine nothing worse and booked myself a hotel elsewhere, while he and the crew enjoyed the sensation of spending the night communing with the ghost of one of the most notorious men in modern history. After our visit, the hotel plans came to nothing, and in 2008 the estate was put up for sale; there were no takers. Today the buildings still stand, now empty and decaying.[16]

When I spoke to Wilfred von Oven in 1991 about our hopes to interview him, he was delighted to revisit Lanke, which he hadn't seen since the autumn of 1944. We filmed him pressing the buttons of the windows. As they parted in the centre and rose and descended before him to reveal the magnificent forest landscape, he cried happily. "It's amazing that I am standing here, pressing these buttons, playing with these windows, and it all works just like fifty years ago. Amazing, fantastic... That I can do it again today is simply wonderful." It was an amazing

---

[16] 14 June 2014
http://www.telegraph.co.uk/news/worldnews/europe/germany/1090 0253/For-sale-the-villa-where-Goebbels-seduced-his-Nazi-starlets.html

scene, as the old Nazi relived his splendid memories. He was a tall, handsome man, even in his late seventies, with a dapper cravat and swept-back grey hair. He told us that his time working for Goebbels had been the highlight of his life. Later we asked him, "If you could sum up your experience of the Third Reich, what would it be?" And he looked back and said, "It was a paradise on earth. For us, it was like that."

Von Oven was an intelligent and thoughtful man, and it was fascinating to hear his version of events. He told me that Goebbels had told him about the concentration camps only in the last days of the regime. "We shouldn't talk about these things," he said. "From the first day of war I was a soldier. The first people to die were slaughtered Germans at Bromberg. These were the first dead. Old women civilians whose heads were smashed in by shovels." This, according to his version, was how the British started the war. In fact, the Bromberg massacre took place two days after the Germans invaded Poland; Germans shot at retreating Polish soldiers, and in the fighting, non-uniformed captured Germans, or possibly civilian ethnic Germans, were killed. However, a quick look at the wilder fringes of the internet confirms von Oven's unlikely theory that some believe that Polish Jews murdered 5,800 German civilians in Bromberg in what became known as Bloody Sunday.[17]

---

[17] www.thefuehrerbunker.com, etc.

As for the concentration camps, von Oven explained to me – correctly – that the British had invented them to contain the Boers in South Africa. Von Oven himself told me that he had had a good friend, "a homosexual called Zamperbauer," who had been held for a while in an early concentration camp in Oranienburg, which was in use from 1933 to 1934, before being replaced in 1936 by Sachsenhausen. At the time, it was more of a detention camp, with forced labour and fences through which the inhabitants could be seen. His friend had told him that conditions were not that bad, and that some of the guards were very attractive and wore sexy boots and uniforms. 'We had a gorgeous Untersturmführer,' he told von Oven. After a fortnight his friend was released. Anyhow, von Oven told me confidentially and confidently, leaning close, "It was never six million."[18] I swallowed and suggested we could split the difference, but that even three million murdered Jews was quite a lot. He shrugged. But he was canny enough not to deny the Holocaust officially and risk prosecution or the threat of not being allowed back into Germany again. In later interviews he would skate close to Holocaust denial before backing away, courteously explaining that he was still a German citizen and had to obey the law. But he would insinuate that many killed Jews were in fact guerrillas fighting behind German lines.[19]

---

[18] "Frau Doktor, es waren kein sechs Million."
[19] For instance, in the *LA Times* interview with Rotella, cited above.

He admired his old boss; "Goebbels knows more than most living men about film,"[20] he later wrote. To me he said, "He was very short, with a big head [von Oven stood over 6ft tall] and he impressed me from the beginning. I love intelligent people." But he was also "quite arrogant and self-important." His life's wish was to be the number two below Hitler; after Hitler's death he was briefly nominated Reichschancellor. It lasted barely two days, but "It was the fulfilment of a dream," said von Oven.

He had clearly discussed the uses and methodology of film propaganda with his old boss. "Goebbels said to me: 'Propaganda is like a convoy in the war which must reach its target under heavy military protection. It must adjust its speed to suit the slowest ship in the flotilla. That's how it is for us too. All sophisticated propaganda is just a waste of time.'"

The propaganda had to be wrapped in entertainment to be digestible and used with a light touch. "He kept telling his film people, 'Just don't bring me any political material. All those political films have turned out dreadfully.'" Von Oven told us how Goebbels briefly banned the Horst Wessel film *Hans Westmar* (which shows young Hans, horrified at decadent Berlin jazz and Jews,

---

[20] This quotation from von Oven's *Finale Furioso: Mit Goebbels bis zum Ende*, Grabert-Verlag, Tübingen 1974, p.36.

fighting and being killed by Communists) and thought that *Hitlerjunge Quex* (which also glorified death in the service of the Nazi party) was also too bluntly didactic. "He knew that. He kept repeating: 'Keep off political films.'" Goebbels rated quality above political correctness and thought an excess of political enthusiasm no excuse for a poor film.[21]

Von Oven claimed, inaccurately, that Goebbels prioritised quality over obeying the race laws, and that of the three hundred film workers that should have been banned for their Jewish heritage, all remained in their posts until the end. He told me that only Fritz Lang and G.W. Pabst emigrated, calmly ignoring other major figures such as Marlene Dietrich, Peter Lorre, Billy Wilder, Robert Siodmak, Hedy Lamarr, Max Ophuls and the hundreds, if not more, less well-known film workers who were forced out of the industry. On the contrary, von Oven said, artists from all over the world, such as Pola

---

[21] "We National Socialists lay no particular value in seeing our SA (storm troopers) marching around on stage or screen. They belong on the streets. However, should somebody try to solve National Socialist problems in art form, they must realise that ambition does not compensate for lack of ability. Even an ostentatious display of a National Socialist attitude is no substitute for the absence of genuine art. The National Socialist government has never demanded the production of SA films. On the contrary: we see danger in this excess. […] In no way does National Socialism justify artistic failure. On the contrary, the greater the idea portrayed, the greater the aesthetic demands." Quoted from Erwin Leiser, *"Deutschland, erwache!" Propaganda im Film des Dritten Reiches* (Reinbek: Rowohlt Verlag, 1968), p.30, author's own translation.

Negri, Kristina Söderbaum and Zara Leander were attracted to Germany. As it happens, Pabst was not Jewish, although he did return to Germany in 1938, spending the rest of the war there; Pola Negri, also probably not Jewish, starred in several German films before fleeing back to America when the Nazis captured France.

Von Oven admired Goebbels' way with the ladies: "Women found him extraordinarily attractive despite his disabled leg. He was elegant and charming. He could, in the most delightful way, make himself agreeable to women."

But he drove his staff, and himself, hard. "He was very demanding at work. By the end of the day you felt pressed out like a lemon." Goebbels himself worked 20-hour days, but he always had a siesta. He was very musical and especially loved baroque music. In public, he had given up smoking, but he continued in secret.

Wilfred von Oven remained at Goebbels' side until 22 April 1945, when Goebbels and his family left for the bunker, where they all died a week later. At that point von Oven left, working briefly for the *Frankfurter Allgemeine Zeitung* under the name of Willy Oehm until his identity was revealed. In 1950, he received his de-Nazification papers and a letter of reference from the editor of *Der Spiegel*, the highly respected Rudolf Augstein, and left for Argentina where he worked briefly as the *Spiegel*'s Argentina correspondent before reverting to more right-wing journals.[22]

After the interview, I left to drive von Oven and his wife to the airport so that they could catch their plane back to Argentina. In the back seat of the car, his wife ripped open the envelope to discover what we had paid them. I had always made it clear it would be a token fee as, so far as I was concerned, the BBC did not pay large sums to old war criminals. In Spanish, they discussed the disappointing amount, and I smiled a little to myself. We then got horribly lost driving through the suburbs of Berlin, and I had this vision of myself—a nice Jewish girl, driving two old Nazis through the town to catch the last flight to Argentina. They caught it with minutes to spare.

I must have hidden my feelings well for, in a follow-up letter to the production office, von Oven wrote. "Please, transmit our hearty greetings to Karen Liebreich whom my wife (and I never disagree with her) considers a really lovely (German: "liebreich") little woman. It would be really nice to see her and her beautiful baby Sam next (European) spring, when we will make our next trip to Europe in order to assist the publishing of my memoirs in Germany." For several years afterwards, I would get

---

[22] Andrea Roepke, Oliver Schroemm, *Stille Hilfe für braune Kameraden: Das geheime Netzwerk der Alt- und Neo-Nazis* (Berlin: Ch. Links Verlag, 2002), pp.132-134.

Christmas cards from Renate and Wilfred, reminding me of our "outstanding example of British-German joint venture" and wishing me a "gutes und liebreiches" New Year.[23] He died in 2008.

* * *

---

[23] Letter to Harriet Rowe at the BBC, 11 October 1992. 1st December 1991, Postcard from Wilfred and Renate von Oven, 'Remembering the outstanding example of British-German joint venture, which happened recently on the former Goebbels ranch near Lanke, grüssen wir unsere[illegible]Prinzessin *with the lucky name* und wünschen ihr ein gutes und liebreiches Jahr 1992.'

Marianne Hoppe

I interviewed Marianne Hoppe in the Akademie der Künste, a central pillar of the Berlin arts establishment. She had shortish brown-blonde hair and a strong, elegant face. She smoked non-stop and talked, very fast with a very complicated vocabulary, in a wonderful rasping voice, although her sentences tended to trail off before completion. Historian David Stewart Hull wrote of her work in the Nazi era, "This actress was the best Germany had to offer."[24] One of the biggest stars of German cinema at the time, she had been married to the film star and director of the Prussian State Theatre under the Third Reich, Gustaf Gründgens, protégé of Hermann Göring. Gründgens' most famous role was as Mephistopheles, the devil who tempts Faust, which he first played in the theatre in 1932. Four years later, at the height of his fame, he married Hoppe.

Gründgens was the subject of a novel written that same year by his ex-brother-in-law Thomas Mann (from his first wife) titled *Mephisto*, which the Nazis had banned before it was finally published in West Germany in 1980. The novel portrayed a thinly disguised Gründgens, who had earlier prided himself on his communist sympathies,

---

[24] David Stewart Hull, *Film in the Third Reich: A study of the German Cinema, 1933-45* (University of California Press, 1969), p.237.

as "an undisguised and thoroughly contemptible opportunist;"[25] it was later adapted as an Oscar-winning film, starring Klaus Maria Brandauer, about a famous gay actor in the Nazi era. Gründgens and his wife hoped and believed that they could somehow remain above politics, dedicated to their art; they ignored the book burnings and the terrible compromises of working with the regime. Gründgens helped a few Jews escape Germany, and he reportedly turned down the anti-Semitic role of *Jud Süß*. However, he starred in many films of the time, rose to an influential and prestigious position as Director of the Berlin State Theatre under the Nazis, frequently socialised with Göring and Goebbels, and moved into a luxurious villa abandoned by a fleeing Jewish banker. Although claiming to be non-partisan, Hoppe and Gründgens lent prestige to the Nazi party and in return were favoured by it; Hoppe occasionally dined with Hitler and played the lead role in several important films, including *Effi Briest* and *Romanze in Moll (Romance in a Minor Key)*. Like so many key artists, Hoppe and Gründgens were on the list of "original geniuses"—the *Gottbegnadetenlisten*—that exempted them from all military or other national service. After the war, investigators judged Hoppe to be "violently Nazi" and closely associated with the NSDAP.[26]

---

[25] Hull, *Film in the Third Reich*, p.91.
[26] Jo Fox, *Filming Women in the Third Reich* (Oxford & New York: Berg, 2000), p.91.

Hoppe told me how she visited the Führer's flat, taking the lift to the fourth floor, where she dined in the company of singer and actress Renate Müller, Leni Riefenstahl, and Späth and his wife. A quick look at those dinner companions provides a potted history of the fate of many under the regime. Hellmut Späth ran a famous plant nursery, one of the largest in the world, and won the valuable landscaping contract for Hitler's new Autobahns. However, he would become increasingly critical of Nazi policies and, in 1945, was executed by firing squad in Sachsenhausen concentration camp; the nursery was closed and the site is now a famous arboretum. Müller, with whom Hitler was infatuated for a short period,[27] had a Jewish lover and refused to work in propaganda films; she later died suddenly, officially from epilepsy but she may have been murdered by the Gestapo or committed suicide to escape them. Leni Riefenstahl, of course, went on to direct some of the regime's most successful films, namely *Olympia* and *Triumph des Willens (Triumph of the Will)*.

Marianne Hoppe admitted that Hitler had charisma. He showed them round his flat, but she said that "in order to be impressed by him, one would have to be an impressionable kind of person already." Of course, she added, she would come to regret the friendship.

---

[27] According to his maid at Berchtesgaden, Pauline Kohler, http://www.libertymagazine.com/war_kohler.htm and a Channel 4 documentary of 2012, *Sex and the Swastika,* Müller had an affair with Hitler, but when Hitler found out about her Jewish lover all was over.

Her relations with Goebbels were more strained. Hoppe's marriage to Gründgens was widely supposed to be a 'lavender marriage', a marriage of convenience to disguise one partner's homosexuality, common among film stars of that era as homosexuality was illegal. Under the Nazis, of course, the penalties were far more severe and for many led to the concentration camp. Goebbels was particularly hostile, dubbing homosexuals '175ers', after the relevant clause in the Weimar constitution which the Nazis had strengthened.[28] After watching *Capriolen*, a 1937 film starring Hoppe and Gründgens, Goebbels wrote in his diary that he had discussed homosexuals with Hitler, who was "adamant: there is no pardon. Rightfully so. We have to clean the theatre of them. And thoroughly." Two weeks later, he wrote that the Berlin State Theatre was a cesspool and "Gründgens must leave the country."[29] But with Göring's protection, he survived and flourished.

Once, Hoppe told me, Goebbels came to her house and rang her doorbell, but she had her lover, the sociologist Carl Dreyfus, in her back room, so she had to get rid of Goebbels without inviting him in. She told me she was never invited to Goebbels' house, but once he warned her husband of a threat to her safety. He showed her a huge cheque, boasting how it represented the royalties he had earned from his book. During the

---

[28] http://www.wsws.org/en/articles/1999/12/gust-d29.html
[29] From Goebbels diaries, 14 and 27 July 1937, cited by Le Faucheur, *Defining Nazi Film*, p.179.

screening of one of her films, *Romanze in Moll*, in 1943, he sat next to her and said not a word all the way through. It told the story of an unhappy woman in a loveless marriage who falls in love with a composer. Eventually, she decides that the only way out is to commit suicide. Hoppe told me she thought that Goebbels probably hated the film, and she was right. He despised it, thinking it defeatist, and presumably—given his own behaviour—believed that women should remain faithful to their husbands whatever the provocation.

In early 1943, she and Gründgens, along with all their actor friends, received an invitation to tea at Goebbels' house, to be followed by a talk at the Sportpalast. She told me they never usually received such invitations, so they knew something serious was afoot. She and Gründgens both claimed that they had dress rehearsals and were unable to attend. They listened to the speech on the radio and were stunned. This was the notorious Total War speech, in which Goebbels demanded a nationwide commitment to the complete mobilisation of economy and society for the war effort. "Total" for Hoppe and her husband meant that they could not continue to work under such conditions. Gründgens rushed upstairs to write a letter to Göring, who was his main protector, begging him to let him go to the front. His request was refused.

In 1944, the regime closed all the theatres. Gründgens and Hoppe received a telegram calling them up on 'film service', the equivalent to military service. They were to make a film called *Das Leben geht weiter* (*Life goes on*). Any actor refusing would be sent to make light bulbs; in reality, there was no choice, explained Hoppe. The film was based on the American film *Mrs Miniver*, starring Greer Garson, the inspirational, award-winning story of an unassuming British housewife forced into heroism by the war. Hoppe was shown the original film in a private screening. She was to play the lead role. She told me she loved the scene where there are thousands of soldiers and women looking for their sons and lovers, and Mrs Miniver's hat is knocked askew as she searches. However, Hoppe said that the actors didn't want to be in this film, which only started filming at the end of 1944, when the military situation was already catastrophic, so she kept pretending to have throat problems and the film was never finished.

In our conversation, she constantly referred to people I had never heard of and rumours with which I was unfamiliar, which made it a tricky interview.[30] She drew a line that was very clear, at least to herself, between

---

[30] Irresistible anecdote about another of Hoppe's lovers: playwright and novelist Ödön von Horváth: After the Anschluss he fled Vienna for Paris. In 1938 he wrote presciently, "I am not so afraid of the Nazis... For instance, I am afraid of streets. Roads can be hostile, can destroy one. Streets scare me. " A few days later he was killed by a falling branch from a tree on the Champs-Elysées.

patriotic films such as *Heideschulmeister Uwe Karsten* (*The Country Schoolmaster*), which emphasised pride in being German, and the more overtly anti-semitic works by directors such as Veit Harlan. Nevertheless, Gründgens' postwar testimony helped to exonerate leading Nazis such as Harlan and Göring's widow. Hoppe was very pleasant and clearly intelligent, but I thought she had little of importance to say about the art of propaganda or Goebbels. She was too keen to exonerate herself. This period was "the black page in my golden book," she told me. "It was just my fate to work in that time."

* * *

Gerhard Huttula

I met Gerhard Huttula at Babelsberg Studios. Two years after the fall of the Berlin Wall, these vast studios, based in Potsdam, an hour southwest of Berlin, faced an uncertain future. To get there, I had to drive past the huge barrier of the old frontier, an impressive monument to Europe's divisions already at that time beginning to be overwhelmed by weeds. The first film was made here in 1911, in what was the oldest large-scale studios in the world, even before they became part of Ufa Germany's near-monopolistic film company. General Erich Ludendorff and the German High Command, together with the director of the Deutsche Bank founded Ufa, Universum Film AG, in 1917, at the height of the First World War, to create war propaganda. "The war has shown the power of images and film," declared the secret foundation memo.[31] In the 1920s, it had become a commercial and artistic powerhouse, with a portfolio that included films such as Josef von Sternberg's *Blaue Engel (The Blue Angel)* starring Marlene Dietrich and Fritz Lang's *Metropolis*, the latter filmed in all three studios, all of which were still in operation when I visited.

---

[31] *Cinema Europe: The Other Hollywood*, 1995, Photoplay Productions for BBC TV series on European silent cinema, written and directed by Kevin Brownlow and David Gill.

Metropolis, released in 1927, was the first film to be inscribed on UNESCO's Register of World Memory and is widely considered to be one of the most influential films of all time. A slight digression: for a previous series on European silent cinema,[32] I tracked down Brigitte Helm, who played the heroine Maria and the iconic robot woman in the film. She married an industrialist of Jewish origin in 1935 and moved to Switzerland, giving up film to bring up her four sons. She was very pleasant on the phone but said that the press always dragged up a traffic accident in which she had been involved, and that she was really just a Swiss housewife and had nothing whatsoever to say about her film career, which had been a very long time ago. She flatly refused to be interviewed.

When we visited Babelsberg in 1991, behind the studios that had once housed the massive futuristic sets of *Metropolis* lay fields and land for outside sets. There were cottages, mud, sheep and donkeys left over apparently from *Pelle the Conqueror*, incongruously sitting alongside Hansel and Gretel's house. There were a few old coaches and a cannon, which someone claimed was the one fired in the 1943 film of *Münchhausen*, and a few pubs, including a frightfully English Ye Olde Bell. Four times a day, there was a kids' show with stunt pirates fighting and falling dramatically. I was shown around the props' store, which included lion skins, flags, seventeenth century paintings,

---

[32] *Cinema Europe.*

ormolu clocks, coats with Jewish stars, deer antlers, costumes and tea cups—everything even including a selection of ceramic kitchen sinks in different sizes and styles.

These studios had been at the heart of Goebbels' film propaganda. After the war, Deutsche Film AG (DEFA) found itself in East Germany, and at the time of my visit the Treuhand—the organisation set up by the German government to find a future and a buyer for various bits of communist property—was in the midst of delicate negotiations. A year later, the French group Compagnie Générale des Eaux would buy Babelsberg and spend millions updating it, creating a world-class film and production company. But when I visited the studios, they had a slightly forlorn look, and the members of staff were uncertain of their futures and keen to showcase the facilities, in spite of the fact that I was researching a film about Nazi cinema.

I negotiated access to a high tower so that we could get an aerial shot of the vast studios and gain an idea of their immense spread. However, when it came to the filming a few weeks later, the cameraman Pat O'Shea, whose main claim to fame was as director of photography and cameraman for *Last of the Summer Wine*, was unable to climb the tower. The BBC had recently been going through one of its periodic series of cutbacks, and cameramen now had no assistants and were forced to carry all their heavy equipment and lights on their own, although the rest of us helped where possible. Although relatively sober at first, by the time we got to Babelsberg studios, Pat was so drunk that we had to abandon the high rise shot. I had spent so much effort requesting access that I was pardonably annoyed.

But all was not wasted. We interviewed Gerhard Huttula, who had been one of Germany's leading cameramen, famed for his special effects. In 1933, he had emigrated to Argentina, but he returned to Germany in 1937 to support his mother and work in Babelsberg. When I interviewed him, he was a spry 89-year old, with blue eyes, white hair, and a slight limp. The studios, he said, were a little golden island where everyone was happy and worked hard. They had unlimited budgets and no military service obligation. They didn't really notice the war, and they didn't have any understanding of "propaganda." The occasional Jew disappeared from work, he volunteered unprompted, but it didn't really affect Huttula's department. Anyhow, he told me, a Jew had once let him down when he was living in Argentina. After a pause and a slightly awkward silence, he added, "On the other hand, a Jew was once helpful to me..."

He never met Goebbels. In fact, he added, the Minister never even visited the studios, which even a quick flick through Goebbels' diaries shows to be far from the truth. But Huttula was busy with his technical marvels and perhaps not important enough at the time to be within Goebbels' range of vision, even though some of his film effects are amongst the most memorable of the period. His most famous achievement was to show actor Hans Albers riding a cannonball in the 1943 film of *Münchhausen*, probably the most famous scene from that film, one of the earliest German colour films.

Münchhausen, "an undisputed masterpiece of European cinema… the greatest German color film of all time,"[33] told the tale of the fictional eighteenth century baron with a gift for hyperbole whose outrageous adventures have delighted readers and viewers for centuries. The film, directed by Josef von Báky and starring the light-hearted and charming Hans Albers, opened at a rococo ball, then followed the baron via the court of Catherine II of Russia, to the seraglio of the sultan in Constantinople, then to Venice where he met Casanova before commandeering a balloon and escaping to the moon. With state-of-the-art colour and technical effects, the film proved hugely popular, with approximately 25 million admissions between 1943 and the end of the war. It has become the German equivalent of its close contemporary, the *Wizard of Oz*, and was supposed to rival Michael Powell and Alexander Korda's *Thief of Baghdad*. Goebbels was delighted with the film, describing it as "an extraordinarily colourful and lively

---

[33]Eric Rentschler, *The Ministry of Illusion: Nazi Cinema and Its Afterlife* (Cambridge: Harvard University Press, 1996), p.196.

fairy-tale picture," which was just as well, since the huge initial budget of 4.57 million Reichsmark was overspent by some two million.[34] Only very few films merited the Agfacolor treatment and expenditure—*Münchhausen* and two Veit Harlan/Kristina Söderbaum films, *Opfergang* and the doomed *Kolberg*. *Münchhausen* featured nudity in the seraglio scenes, unusual at the time, and its comedy and pure escapism encapsulated its aims. Viewers could go to the cinema, forget their troubles, forget that they were living in difficult and dangerous times, and simply laugh and enjoy.

Hans Albers' cannonball flight, created by Huttula, is a striking and lasting image. One historian calls it the "cinematic equivalent of a V-2 rocket" and claims "the famous image of Hans Albers seated on a cannonball flying through the sky essentializes the nexus between cinema's powers of illusion and war's tools of aggression."[35] For Huttula, however, it was simply a technical challenge to be overcome.

Huttula also excelled in aerial dogfights, such as those in *Quax, der Bruchpilot (1941)*, and Göring absolutely adored his Stuka fight scenes. Occasionally the filmmakers would be invited by "a higher authority" to watch American films, such as *Captains Courageous*, a coming-of-age film featuring exciting sea scenes with Spencer Tracy

---

[34] Rentschler, *Ministry of Illusion*, p.197.
[35] Rentschler, *Ministry of Illusion*, p.203.

crashing to his death from splintering masts into the foaming seas. These would be private screenings, organised under high security, and designed to keep German filmmakers abreast of the latest Hollywood techniques. There was always plenty of money for their work, said Huttula, although during the war it was sometimes hard to get materials.

Huttula may have become "one of Germany's most accomplished optical and process cinematographers,"[36] but he was not a reliable interviewee. He claimed to me that *Jud Süß* by common consent now considered "one of the most notorious and successful pieces of anti-Semitic film propaganda produced in Nazi Germany,"[37] had never been shown in the cinema and that it had been very unpopular as people wanted escapism and fun. In fact, it was a box office hit. Huttula later worked with the director of *Jud Süß*, Veit Harlan, on *Opfergang*, a gloomy tale of sacrifice and death.

Harlan's next film, on which Huttula also worked, was *Kolberg*, a ludicrously big budget spectacular that deployed thousands of soldiers as extras and brought in a hundred trainloads of salt to film the snowy winter scenes

---

[36] Rolf Glesen, J.P.Storm, *Animation under the Swastika: A History of Trickfilm in Nazi Germany, 1933-1945* (Jefferson: McFarland, 2012).

[37] Nicholas John Cull; David Holbrook Culbert; David Welch, *Propaganda and Mass Persuasion: A Historical Encyclopedia, 1500 to the present* (Santa Barbara: ABC-CLIO, 2003), p. 205. Retrieved 27 October 2011, from Wikipedia entry.

in summer—all this in 1944 as the Third Reich was crumbling to complete defeat. It told of the heroic resistance unto death of a Prussian town during the Napoleonic invasion, despite the surrender of local officials. It cost eight times more than any other German film of its time and involved some 187,000 extras. It was a project dear to Goebbels' heart, and the propaganda echoes must have been very clear to the director, Harlan. Later, Harlan wrote that "Hitler as well as Goebbels must have been obsessed with the idea that a film like this could be more useful to them than even a victory in Russia."[38] For Huttula, however, there was no connection with the politics of the time. No propaganda tricks were used in the filming of *Kolberg*, he told me, and when I suggested there might have been a connection between the military and political situation of Germany in 1944 and *Kolberg* in 1806, he seemed astonished. For him, it was just a couple of days' holiday at the seaside, and he didn't even read the whole scenario, just his own scenes. Although obviously, he conceded, Harlan must have got the battalions of soldiers to participate because of his "high-up contacts."

Gerhard Huttula was one of those passengers who basically approved of the regime and was not particularly curious about its wider ramifications. He did his bit, and he did it well, a technician who looked no

---

[38] Quoted in David Weinberg, "Approaches to the Study of Film in the Third Reich: A Critical Appraisal," *Journal of Contemporary History*, vol.19, no.1 (Jan 1984) pp.105-126, p.114.

further beyond his own sphere of expertise. He didn't bother to read the whole script—neither of his films, nor of his politics. And after the war, after a few years of theatre set building, he slotted back into his film work, initially working on children's films and then adverts.

* * *

Rudolf Klicks

Our final interview at Babelsberg was with Rudolf Klicks, a dapper, compact little man who had been a young actor in films such as the 1934 *Die Reiter von Deutsch-Ostafrika (The Riders of German East Africa)*, where he played a heroic young volunteer who is shot supplying water to German farmers oppressed by the British colonialists. Ironically, the film was banned both by the Nazis, in 1939, for being too pacifist, and by the Allies, after the war, for being too militaristic. Described by one film historian as "the German Micky Rooney of the period,"[39] Klicks became a film photographer, trick cameraman and assistant film editor (more or less a film censor under the Nazis) as his status as a youth star faded. He was keen to be interviewed in English, being very proud of his mastery of the language, but his English was both inaccurate and speedy, so that he ended up sounding like a series of eponymous clicks, which made it difficult to understand him. For Klicks, just like for von Oven, his time at Babelsberg, war or no war, was the best time of his life. "This place in Germany, Babelsberg, was the greatest place for film in the whole of Europe... It was a beautiful time; it was a magnet because everybody was like one great family. Whether it was a simple worker or the

---

[39] David Stewart Hull, *Film in the Third Reich: A Study of the German Cinema 1933-1945* (University of California Press, 1969), p.59.

highest director this was one group working [together] in the beautiful atmosphere of film. It was the dream of everyone's life." He sighed nostalgically. It may have been one happy family for Klicks, but the day after Goebbels' famous meeting with the film industry in the Hotel Kaiserhof, in March 1933, the Board of Directors of Ufa announced: 'With regard to the question raised by Germany's national revolution concerning Ufa's further engagement of Jewish workers and staff, the board of directors has resolved to revoke as far as possible its contracts with Jewish personnel.'[40] Well ahead of schedule, Ufa managers compiled a list and within an hour "actors, producers, composers, authors, and technical specialists"[41] were fired. By 1938, the film industry was officially considered purified, *Juden-frei*, Jew-free. From 12 November 1938, Jews were no longer even allowed to visit cinemas to watch films. So much for family loyalty.

* * *

---

[40] moviemoviesite.com/articles/events/enemies_of_the_state/page_1.htm
[41] Klaus Kreimeier, *The Ufa Story: A History of Germany's Greatest Film Company, 1918-1945* (University of California Press, 1999), p.211.

Erich Kästner

Wherever you see film crews around the world today, you often see a big truck with ARRI written all over it. This stands for August Arnold and Robert Richter (hence the name AR-RI), who went to school together, and in 1917, while still teenagers, opened a small shop in Türkenstrasse in the Schwabing district of Munich, which is still the headquarters of ARRI industries.

Erich Kästner—not the man of the same name and period who was the author of *Emil and the Detectives*—was one of ARRI's longest-serving employees. He invented the first single reflex camera, the Arriflex 35, which was presented at the Leipzig Exhibition of 1937 and changed the film industry throughout the world. His major breakthrough was to get rid of the parallax, so that what the cameraman saw through the viewfinder reflected the actual image to be filmed rather than a view somewhere next to the actual image; this sounds so obvious to us now that any alternative is unthinkable. Today's cameras still use this technology, and in 1982, Kästner was awarded an Oscar "for the concept and engineering of the first operational 35mm handheld, spinning-mirror reflex motion picture camera."

Goebbels attended the Leipzig show and came to the stand to inspect the camera that had caused so much interest. Later, he asked August Arnold to visit him in his office for a private demonstration. Without Kästner's invention, the wartime propaganda newsreels, the rousing speeches by Nazi leaders, Leni Riefenstahl's films would all have been very different. The new Arri cameras were also very small and light and were to prove especially good for war reporting. The film cassettes could be changed quickly, another major advantage in the field. The first one was sold in March 1938, and the war proved very good business for them. Some seventy years later, around 60 per cent of all major feature films still used Arri cameras.[42] Two years after our interview, he would win another Oscar for lifetime achievement.

I met Kästner in the Arri offices in Munich surrounded by original old cameras, many of them designed by him. He let me hold the Oscar that he had won for technical achievement, and it was surprisingly heavy. He looked very old and a little vague, but once he took up a pencil and paper and started to describe his technical breakthroughs, he became precise and coherent. He told me how, under pressure from a cameraman, Otto Josef Wirsching, he had started work on the reflex camera. Leni Riefenstahl would later claim it had been done at her insistence, but Kästner told me he had been planning it

---

[42] Article by Thomas Schuler, *The Atlantic Times*, May 2008.
http://www.atlantic-times.com/archive_detail.php?recordID=1312

from as early as 1932, while Riefenstahl was only just beginning to work her way from the front to the back of the camera, from romantic film heroine to acclaimed director.

When we came to film this interview, it proved disastrous. Pat O'Shea, our troublesome cameraman, was initially interested in the technical angle and chatted away knowledgeably to the bewildered inventor. Then, as we began filming, he fell asleep over his camera while I struggled to keep the interview going. The director would keep an eye on his monitor and prod Pat awake again as the burly cameraman settled his somnolent weight over the barrel of his camera, and the old German disappeared either upwards or downwards off the screen, depending on Pat's weight distribution over the camera. Meanwhile, the microphone was filled with Pat's deep snores. It was very trying and the footage was unusable.

* * *

Brigitte Mira and Margot Hielscher

I interviewed two ageing film stars, Brigitte Mira and Margot Hielscher, both of whom were at the time appearing at the Theater des Westens in a dull production of Stephen Sondheim's *Follies*. Mira's changing room was filled with curlers, children's cuddly toys and a nasty little fluffy dog, Tiffany. Mira was short and fat, with brassy red hair, unattractive, but very colourful. In recent years, she had dubbed the German voice for *When the Wind Blows* and had become famous as a cleaning lady in Fassbinder films. She seemed to me to be thick as a plank, vain and unable to concentrate. She saw herself as a big star, glamorous and fascinating, and was keen to tell me all about herself and Fassbinder; unfortunately, I only wanted to know about her work under the Third Reich. Ironically, she was half Jewish, but she had survived the Nazi regime under forged papers. She starred in a series of propaganda shorts titled *Liese und Miese*, about two girls, a good quiet one (Liese) and a naughty one, Miese, played by Mira. Miese criticised the government, hoarded rationed food, failed to observe the blackout, and let slip crucial information to listening spies, while the good Liese obeyed government instructions to the letter. Apparently Goebbels hated the films as they showed criticism of the regime, and after ten episodes, they were cancelled. It seems Mira's character was too funny and sympathetic. I personally found her unsympathetic and uninteresting, and we did not interview her on film.

I decided to concentrate on Margot Hielscher instead, a few changing rooms further down the corridor of the Theater des Westens. A singer and general forces' sweetheart during the war, she had reportedly had a romantic liaison with Goebbels. She was still a large-eyed, striking and very well-preserved brunette. The director was excited to talk to a woman who had actually experienced the Gauleiter's famous casting couch, resulting initially in a small role as handmaid to Mary Queen of Scots in an anti-English wartime film of 1940, *Das Herz der Königin (The Queen's Heart),* but of course Hielscher was keen to be remembered for other things. Luckily she spoke excellent English, so he was able to question her himself instead of via my embarrassed translation. The highlight of her career (apart from reportedly sleeping with Goebbels), was two appearances representing Germany at the Eurovision Song Contest; she achieved a creditable fourth place in 1957. She also had an unmemorable role in *The Vikings* with Tony Curtis and Kirk Douglas.

Babelsberg was the centre of her world during the early 1940s. "It was very glamorous, and it was very very big and being a newcomer in my case, I of course adored every little corner. It was so much alive with so many brilliant directors, actors, actresses and cameramen. The atmosphere was hard to describe. It was so alive and so important and so overwhelming."

As for Goebbels: "He had all the influence you can imagine. He had to say who was getting a part or not. Whenever a director said he would like to have Margot Hielscher, he had to say yes. If he had said no, I wouldn't have gotten the part. His influence was just endless."

"He was very charming. You very seldom find the possibility to say a man has charm—like Maurice Chevalier or some of the big movie stars who have charm, but he had charm; he was very charming. He knew how to handle a woman." The thought of Goebbels as a German Chevalier provided a novel insight.

Hielscher had an amusing anecdote to tell about his amorous pursuit of her. "He called at night, very late—eleven o'clock, sometimes close to midnight, and he always called himself Herr Müller. The telephone was in my father's room, so he answered the phone, and he came to our room where Anita, my sister, and I were sleeping, and he said, 'This Mr Müller wants to talk to you. I have the terrible feeling this is not Mr Müller at all; this sounds like Goebbels.' And it was Goebbels!"

Hielscher claimed she repelled his advances, but later Kristina Söderbaum assured me that she had proof that Hielscher had succumbed. At any rate she must have fallen from favour fairly speedily, as she didn't get any further starring roles.

* * *

Theodor Nischwitz and Lida Baarova

I met with a very pleasant old gentleman, Theodor Nischwitz. He invited me to dinner, and I threw up the whole night afterwards.

Nischwitz started as a trainee trick cameraman under Gerhard Huttula. They worked together on a film called *Amphitryon* in 1935. Jupiter fancies a Theban woman, Alcmene, but fails to seduce her as his aged self, so he disguises himself as her husband, Amphitryon, and has another go. Later, Alcmene produces twin boys, one of whom, Hercules, is the son of Jupiter, the other the son of her husband. Nischwitz worked on the scenes in which the gods wear roller skates and Jupiter wore horns, and it was his task to create the effect of electrical current flashing from the god's face. "It was my favourite film, a work of art," he told me. It was a light fluffy comedy and generally well received. Nischwitz then worked on *Es war eine rauschende Ballnacht* (*It was a Gay Ballnight*), for which his job was to make the waltzing lovers fly through the air.

Nischwitz's next job was on *Barcarole*, named for the folk song sung by Venetian gondoliers. He told me that the required gondolas proved so hard to steer that Italian gondoliers had to be imported, whereupon the girls fell in love with them and caused all sorts of distractions. The film was most notable for providing the debut role for Lida Baarova, a Czech actress with whom Goebbels fell in love. Nischwitz remembered Goebbels visiting the studio in 1935 to watch Baarova's filming. Goebbels noted in his diary that the film was not of interest, but the actress was. The Propaganda Minister was famous for his casting couch lustfulness, but this affair with Baarova, a slim, dark-haired beauty, was more serious, and Goebbels contemplated leaving his wife for her.

At the time, Baarova was living with her co-star Gustav Fröhlich in Schwanenwerder, near Lanke. She first met Goebbels in the company of one of his daughters; the minister invited her onto his yacht. She usually went to watch Fröhlich work, but that evening Goebbels intervened, so she stayed, and they swam and dined, and, in short, had a wonderful evening.[43]

"I was never very secure with Fröhlich," she said years later in an interview. "But Goebbels was very open with me and praised me, and I became a better actress from this." While others, Leni Riefenstahl for instance, complained that the Minister was a groper, Baarova found his behaviour that of a gentleman. "He was very witty and could be very sarcastic, he imitated his colleagues," she

---

[43] *Joseph Goebbels, gesehen von der UFA-Star, Lida Baarova*, film by Werner Koch and Günter Krause, WDR 1991.

said. "We laughed a lot and understood each other very well. Many people say he was a devil, but he was never like that to me; to me, he was always terribly nice."

Meanwhile, Fröhlich, as Goebbels' rival, found his star exemption from military service summarily lifted, and he was told to report for military service. Director Veit Harlan added fuel to the fire by calling Fröhlich "un-German and revolting."[44]

The affair continued for two blissful years. Film roles came her way. "I just saw that everyone worked, and everyone had a villa. I had no villa and only a BMW. He would have given me things, but I didn't want anything. He really loved me."

The young actress was overwhelmed. "I loved him in my own way, I was very young. You mustn't forget, I was only twenty-two years old, and one is very susceptible to such things at that time. I actually loved his love for me. He loved me so very much that I fell in love with his love."

Eventually Goebbels' wife Magda contacted the actress and dictated some terms to her: "You love my husband. So do I. He's a genius, and he needs both of us.

---

[44] Jana Francesca Bruns, *Nazi Cinema's New Women* (Cambridge: Cambridge University Press, 2009), p.40.

In my house he's mine, outside I don't care. Only don't have a child." Baarova hoped to leave for Hollywood, but Magda was afraid Goebbels might follow her. Things came to head one evening when Magda invited Baarova over for the weekend. In the evening they were to watch a film—Magda wanted a film starring Anny Ondra, Goebbels insisted on *Der Spieler*, starring Baarova. The next day, Magda went to ask Hitler to intervene.

At first, the Minister held out. Baarova said: "Goebbels wanted to resign and go to Japan as consul. He said, even if I have to sell ties in Japan, I don't care, I want to resign. But Hitler made a terrible scene. Hitler was angry because of course he needed Goebbels. Hitler wouldn't accept Goebbels' resignation and said, all right try living with your wife for three months more. If after three months you come to me and say you can't live together, then I will give you a divorce. Naturally he didn't mean it, he only wanted to gain time." The strategy worked. Goebbels telephoned Baarova, with Goering sitting next to him to ensure compliance. In 1938, on Hitler's direct order, Berlin's head of police told Baarova to leave Germany. The Hollywood offer was no longer on the table. She fled at night, via the window and dark side streets, first to Prague and later to Italy. "Sometimes I was unhappy," she said, "but I couldn't really escape. He used to 'phone me, in Salzburg, in Viareggio, in St Moritz…. I was so lonely, I couldn't talk to anyone. I had to sort it out alone, but I was too young. Not to exculpate myself, but it was a mistake, I just fell into the situation and I couldn't get out."[45] In the final days of the Reich, around the 18 or 20 April 1945, Wilfred von Oven was helping Goebbels to destroy his papers. Goebbels sat at his desk, emptying the drawers, and he pulled out a large still of Baarova and showed it to his assistant. Then he tore it across four times and handed the little pieces to von Oven to burn. "It was the final farewell," said von Oven.

Theodor Nischwitz, the cameraman, meanwhile, was on holiday in Yugoslavia when war broke out, so he was unable to arrange his release from the army. He was sent to Russia as a war cameraman, equipped with a large 1000mm Ascania for long shots and a smaller Arri camera for the close ups. He loved his Arri camera—the clever new lenses meant that the cameraman could be sure to have the whole person in shot, while it was much easier to load, an important attribute in the freezing Russian temperatures. It was so cold, minus 18 degrees, that they had to keep their Arris warm under their pillows, and people wore everything, including tea cosies, to keep warm. In November 1941, Nischwitz said he was sent over from Talinn to film the aftermath of a terrible disaster. The Russian Navy had been surrounded in Talinn in August that year and had been forced to evacuate via mine-strewn sea lanes. A passenger ship with 3,000 Russian soldiers, women and children hit a German mine,

---

[45] All quotations from Baarova taken from WDR film interview.

he told me, while trying to break through from Finland to Leningrad. Thousands were drowned and burnt and some of the survivors then killed themselves. Nischwitz described filming the bodies turning slowly on the ropes from which they had hanged themselves, gradually becoming covered in snow. The injured living, including children still clutching their toys, were laid on steel plates on the deck, and some froze onto the metal, still alive and suffering. Even fifty years later, he seemed traumatised by the terrible sights he had filmed, but he said he had rarely seen his work as he was at the front. When I pointed out that none of this footage would have been screened, since it showed Russian children killed in a terrible way by a German mine, he looked shocked.

When his camera broke soon afterwards, he was flown back for some leave. Then, along with two other cameramen, he was sent to the western front to film *Westwall*, directed by Fritz Hippler. Hippler later filmed one of the most notorious of anti-Jewish films, *Der Ewige Jud* (*The Eternal Jew*) and we interviewed him too. For the film *Westwall*, they filmed sections of the Siegfried Line (the Westwall) very carefully, in order to show that the line remained intact. When I said that that probably counted as effective propaganda, he again looked astonished. "Good gracious, I never thought of that before!"

Nischwitz's next job was to make three captured Russian planes look like thirty for a Luftwaffe paean of praise called *Stukas*. From there he moved on in 1943 to *Münchhausen*, the jolly fantasy film on which Huttula had also worked, where Nischwitz's task was to work on the speed running scene, which he did by choosing every fourth or sixth frame so that the magical runner could sprint superfast to save the Baron. The skill, he told me, was to get the angle and the speed to match. This film too played a key part of Goebbels' propaganda empire, aimed at getting people to forget their troubles while watching magical and humorous whimsy.

After this pleasant interlude, Nischwitz was sent back to the Russian Front, to Minsk. He explained how minutely the Propaganda Ministry controlled their work, with memos criticising their film techniques—this scene was over-lit, that was too wobbly, they shouldn't focus on the sexy girls... Before Stalingrad, they received a memo ordering them only to film soldiers advancing from left to right, attacking from Germany towards the enemy on the eastern front. After the defeat at Stalingrad, they were told to focus on people gritting their teeth and holding on.

After the war Nischwitz worked with Fassbinder on *Berlin Alexanderplatz* and with Wolfgang Petersen on the highly successful drama *Das Boot*. It seemed to me that he was a pure craftsman who was astonished to discover that some of his work could be considered propaganda. He had simply filmed what he was asked to film, and he had spent most of the war either on the Russian front or making harmless entertainment films. I enjoyed our dinner together.

***

Fritz Hippler

We also interviewed Fritz Hippler for the programme, in his house overlooking Berchtesgaden and Hitler's mountain lodge.[46] Head of Goebbels' film department (Reichsfilmdramaturg) between 1939 and 1943, Hippler directed the repellent *Der Ewige Jud* (*The Eternal Jew*). According to Erik Barnouw, Hippler produced the anti-Semitic film that Goebbels requested in "spectacularly odious fashion."[47] The film consists of a five-pronged attack against the Jews: they are personally repellent, threateningly assimilationist, financially powerful, culturally pernicious and religiously alien. The typical Jew, claims the film, wallows in dirt, is materialistic, and never truly creative but imitative. The ability of Jews to assimilate themselves is terrifying for the rest of society—Hippler cuts between full screens showing packs of rats scurrying around and devouring grain, and degenerate-looking groups of seedy Jewish men clad in dirty black, before mounting a crude attack on all stereotypical aspects of international Jewry. He used excerpts from fiction films, such as *The House of Rothschild* and material shot in the Warsaw Ghetto, to emphasise the way Jews

---

[46] I didn't interview Hippler myself, but the footage was shot for and used in our programme.
[47] Erik Barnouw, *Documentary: A History of the Non-fiction Film*, Oxford University Press, 1983), p.141.

supposedly manipulate international finance, create wars, barter old rags and follow archaic and brutal religious practices. Hippler told us: "With this film Hitler wanted to prove that the Jews were a parasitic race within mankind that had to be separated from the rest of mankind. That was what this film was supposed to prove."

Goebbels looked at the rushes and his diary entry reveals him to be so repelled as to be almost exhilarated: "Hippler back from Poland with a lot of material for the ghetto film... The Jew film... Never seen anything like it. Scenes so horrific and brutal in their explicitness that one's blood runs cold. One shudders at such barbarism. This Jewry must be eliminated."[48]

The editing of the rushes took over a year and proved tricky. Hippler remembered the process as being painful: "Over a period of thirteen months this film was re-arranged at least a dozen times. It was changed, re-cut and added to, not to mention the various versions of the accompanying text which grew progressively more bloodthirsty and aggressive."

---

[48] Entry for 17 October 1939. See also Diary 17, 24, 28 October 1939; 2, 11, 19 November 1939; 18 December 1939, 9, 12 January 1940, 11 October 1940.

Der Ewige Jud finally opened in autumn 1940 and ran in sixty-six Berlin cinemas simultaneously.[49] It received its premiere in Berlin two months after *Jud Süß* and was far less successful. Attendance figures fell sharply after the grand opening. People were observed leaving the cinema in disgust in the middle of the performance, finding it too repulsive.[50]

Fritz Hippler was one of the least charming and most convinced Nazis we interviewed, and I wasn't sorry to have missed the trip.

---

[49] Ian Kershaw, *Popular Opinion and Political Dissent in the Third Reich: Bavaria 1933-1945* (Oxford UniversityPress, 2002), p.364.
[50] Report from the Federal Archive, Koblenz. R 58/157, pp.7-9 dated 20 January 1941.

Brunhilde Pomsel

In 2011, *Bild Zeitung*[51] hailed an "exclusive interview" with Brunhilde Pomsel, claiming that it was the first time she had spoken since the war, but they got very little from her. By then she was one hundred years old. She said she had been obliged to take the job in Goebbels' office because she had been one of the fastest typists at the Berliner Rundfunk and that she had earned 500 Reichsmark per month. She recalled that every day someone came to give Goebbels a manicure. She said she knew nothing of the worst aspects of the Nazi regime, such as the policy towards the Jews. "I was a silly, politically uninterested sausage with simple relationships. The first I heard of it was after I was released from prison." She spent the last ten days of the war in the cellar at the Propaganda Ministry, where office business continued. She heard about her boss's suicide on 1 May 1945, and spent the next five years in a Russian prison. "I'll never forgive Goebbels for what he did in the world. And that he let his innocent children be killed," she told *Bild*.

Between 1933 and 1942, she was a secretary in the news department of the Reich Radio Broadcasting in Berlin. Then she spent the next three years of the war in

---

[51] 23 August 2011, http://www.bild.de/regional/muenchen/joseph-goebbels/seine-sekretaerin-im-interview-19534892.bild.html

the Propaganda Ministry, in the Minister's office. Between 1945 and 1950, she was in a Russian prison camp, and from there she returned to work in German broadcasting, for SWF in Baden-Baden.

The *Daily Beast, Daily Mail* and others picked up on the story, announcing that Pomsel had "broken a 66-year long vow of silence... Since the end of World War II, Brunhilde Pomsel, now 100, has refused all requests for interviews and offers to publish her memoirs."[52] I first interviewed her on 3 October 1991 at her flat in Ansprengerstrasse 25 in Munich. It was the first time she had ever spoken of her wartime experience. She was a chirpy little grey-haired sparrow of a lady, with a brisk manner and sharp eyes behind glasses. The window sills of her flat were filled with bright geraniums, and she baked me some delicious biscuits. We sat and had a nice coffee and a chat, a real *Kaffeeklatsch*. I thought how surreal it was—me, the daughter of a Holocaust survivor, drinking coffee with Goebbels' typist. At the age of 105, still sharp and unremorseful, Pomsel gave a series of interviews to a film-maker explaining how basically "I didn't do anything

---

52

http://www.thedailybeast.com/articles/2011/08/30/goebbels-secretary-brunhilde-pomsel-secrets-of-nazi-secretaries.html
http://www.dailymail.co.uk/news/article-2031365/Goebbels-secretary-100-breaks-silence-cold-distant-monster-Germans-hate-Jews.html

other than type in Goebbels's office."[53] She died a few months later, on 27 January 2017.[54]

Brunhilde Pomsel worked for the Propaganda Ministry from 1942 to 1945. She sat in the front room with three or four other secretaries doing the typing. Joseph Goebbels also had a private secretary for his diaries and personal appointments. When he arrived at work, he would slip past the girls quietly, but when he left, they would acknowledge him formally. He was polite, though reserved. He never chased the secretaries, although several were very pretty, reserving his attentions for actresses. Pomsel thought he had a kind of inferiority complex because of his club foot, so the power he had achieved through the regime was particularly important to him.

While she found Hitler very unattractive—"a very ugly little man"—with a horrid voice, Pomsel found Goebbels more appealing. "He had a handsome face, he was always very beautifully well-dressed. Of course, he was a bit short," she admitted, "but had he been 20cm taller I could really have fancied him." Twenty years later she told *Bild* that he was a cold and distant monster.[55]

---

[53] https://www.theguardian.com/world/2016/aug/15/brunhilde-pomsel-nazi-joseph-goebbels-propaganda-machine
[54] This chapter appeared on Pomsel's death in *London Review of Books*, February 2017.
[55] *Daily Mail*, 29 August 2011.

Pomsel never saw her boss's wife in the office, although when she was bombed out and her possessions destroyed, Magda Goebbels sent her a really nice dress. She went to dinner a few times at Goebbels' place in Schwanenwerder. When Goebbels gave his famous Total War speech in February 1943, after the battle for Stalingrad, he ordered the office staff to attend, and Pomsel sat directly behind Magda.

The atmosphere in the office changed markedly after Stalingrad. Pomsel thought that Goebbels realised from then on that Germany would lose the war, but he was so bound up with Nazism that he could not escape; there was no possibility of surrender for him. The ordinary people, like Pomsel herself, who got their information from the weekly *Wochenschau* film news bulletins, still believed they could win. She couldn't believe the leadership would have continued if they didn't have some kind of secret weapon up their sleeves.

She remembered a screening of *Kolberg* at the office on 17 April 1945, in the very last days of the Reich. It had a kind of public relations message, she told me: We must stay strong and we'll win. Goebbels saw himself playing a role in a future film very similar to this one. "Hold out now," he wrote "so that a hundred years hence the audience does not hoot and whistle when you appear on the screen."[56]

As for *Jud Süß*, it was a good film, she said with some relish. Was it anti-Jewish? Maybe, she admitted, "But it was really well made." Pomsel herself wasn't anti-Semitic, she told me (as so many Nazis did). "I had a Jewish friend called Ewa Löwenthal. I didn't see her for a while, then I met her on the bus. I told her I was working at the Propaganda Ministry. Ewa joked, she should come by and visit me there. I said, 'Well, really! Better not.' ['*Um Gottes Himmel, Ewa, nein!*'] I never saw her again. It was very sad." I usually remained neutral in my interviews, but at this I could not resist pointing out that Ewa had most probably been killed, as most Jews were, and Pomsel looked a little surprised and uncomfortable. I thought she had perhaps never before considered that the gassed Jews, the *Untermenschen*, were real people that she might actually know, that one of them might even have been a friend. At any rate, Ewa's death was nothing to do with Fraülein Pomsel. She was the kind of thoughtless 'fellow traveller' who one could easily imagine checking the spelling of Zyklon B in her typing manual without thinking through any further ramifications. It was only in 2005, when Berlin finally opened its Holocaust Memorial, that Pomsel finally went to check her friend's fate, only to discover that,

---

[56] Quoted in David Welch, *Propaganda and the German Cinema, 1933-1945* (London: I.B. Tauris, 2001) p.197.

predictably, she had been deported to Auschwitz in November 1943 and was never again seen alive.

Pomsel used to see the Goebbels children when she worked on Saturdays. "They were so sweet and well-behaved... The children were delightful with no trace of arrogance. Very nice, pleasant, well brought up children." Everyone commented on Goebbels' children. Wilfred von Oven told me they were gorgeous, five little girls and one boy, each one cuter and cleverer than the other. He recalled them in the country house at Lanke, "in a row, like organ pipes. I'll never forget them, all in little white frocks. The eldest two were dark, the next three very blonde. My favourite was Helmut; he was not as bright as the girls."

Of all the things that Goebbels may have done, Pomsel cannot forgive him for ordering the murder of his children in the bunker as the Russians advanced. An SS doctor sedated the children, aged between four and twelve years old, and Magda then went into the room to crush cyanide capsules between their teeth. Unequal to the task, she called on Hitler's personal doctor to help her finish the job. Magda and Goebbels then killed themselves. Maybe, Pomsel said in a faint effort to explain their loving father's actions, he became a victim of his own propaganda on Russian atrocities.

Pomsel enjoyed her work. She claims to have been politically uninterested, and when I asked whether she regretted anything she did, she said, "Why should I, I was just typing." Later she added that perhaps she should have been more thoughtful. But anyhow after the war she spent five years in a Russian labour camp, "which was very unfair." If anything, she regretted having stayed at her post, sorting out and filing memos, to the bitter end.

* * *

Hans-Otto Meissner

Hans-Otto Meissner was the son of Otto Meissner, head of the office of the President of Germany during the Weimar Republic and the longest serving Secretary of State, serving Paul von Hindenburg for many years. Otto had played a key role in the appointment of Hitler to the post of Chancellor and in 1937, he became state minister and chief of the presidential chancellery of the Führer. His son, my interviewee Hans-Otto, was born in 1909. In 1933, Meissner Jr. joined the SS, and in 1934, he became an attaché in the diplomatic service, serving in London and Tokyo. On the outbreak of war, he was transferred to work on military news and the propaganda service and from 1940 served in the German Embassy in Moscow. From 1941-45, he was consul in Milan and involved in anti-Jewish activities. At the end of the war, the Americans briefly imprisoned and then released him; his own view was that they let him go because of a personal intervention by the controversial Pope Pius XII, who had become a family friend during his period as Papal Nuncio. After the war, Meissner worked successfully as a writer and journalist, receiving several establishment honours and penning 75 mediocre books of travel, memoirs, hunting and second-rate biographies, including one of Magda Goebbels.

I met the self-declared Big Game Hunter, now aged 82, at his forest lodge, Jagdhaus Siebenschlaf, in Unterwossen, 80km south-west of Munich. Outside fluttered the large flag of the erstwhile monarch of Bavaria. Meissner wore a traditional felt loden coat with antler buttons, and he and his wife looked plump and well fed. We chatted before a backdrop of dead animals, a gruesome spectacle that included two polar bears, two wolves, several foxes, many large birds and a whole African game park of rare and dead beasts. There were perhaps 400 deer antlers covering the walls. The host had personally shot all of them. One room was decorated completely with a carpet made of deerskin. Any small spaces on the walls between the dead animals were filled with photos of "me with the Shah of Persia", "me with Cardinal Ratzinger", "me with Josef Strauss" (the corrupt minister-president of Bavaria who dropped dead while hunting in 1988), a roll call of compromised conservative leaders. His first question was to ask how much money we would pay for the interview. I assured him that the payment would be a piffling goodwill gesture, but his vanity was such that he agreed to the interview anyway. His English was excellent.

We ate dinner, and I remember looking at the gravy running down his slobbery chin and the glassy eyes of the hundreds of dead animals all around us and wondering what the fuck I was doing there. My gorge rose, and only the thought of skewering the rich unpleasant old fool in an interview for posterity kept me sitting there breaking bread with him. Certainly he was living proof that a Nazi background was no disadvantage in post-war Germany.

He told me of his family background and assured me that he and his parents always moved in the best—or worst—circles. He showed me photos of his parents with Joseph and Magda Goebbels, which we could use—for an extra charge, of course. Meissner remembers his mother asking Goebbels, "How come you have so many houses when you say people should live austerely?" He replied, "You should be too intelligent to believe anything I say!" Meissner's father, according to my host, represented the decent old Prussian type, so Goebbels hated him.

Meissner told me that Goebbels was very charming and spoke very well. "He didn't believe in Nazism," he said. "He had no conscience, and was only anti-Semitic because it was politic. He had no power base of his own such as the SS or the SA; he depended entirely on Hitler."

Meissner used to belong to an Artists' Club in Berlin, and he remembered seeing Goebbels there with girls on his lap and his hand up their blouse. He used to sleep with girls in his house too, and he had sex with many women, including Ello Quandt, Magda's sister-in-law by her previous marriage. Ello told Meissner this in confidence; she later became the main source for his 1978 biography of Magda. Ello—and Meissner—were sympathetic to Magda, seeing her as a victim of Goebbels' propaganda.

He was less fond of Leni Riefenstahl, whom he constantly referred to as the "Reich's glacier crevasse" (Reichsgletscherspalte), after her starring roles in various ski and mountain films in the late 'twenties and early 'thirties. Meissner came across her in September 1939 in Poland, where she was filming weekly newsreel—*Wochenschau*—reports. He told me how she insisted on crossing a bridge with her three Mercedes, and when the commander tried to refuse her access, Meissner heard her saying she would phone Goebbels and Hitler directly to get permission over his head. He said this showed that she was in close contact with Goebbels, in spite of her frequent denials. It was on this trip that she witnessed the execution of Polish Jews, which apparently upset her so much that she stopped filming for, well, almost two weeks.

For Meissner, however, the treatment of the Jews was not an issue. "Of course, the Jews could leave at any time and take all their money. Many of them survived the war in Germany throughout." I didn't even bother to ask him whether he had any regrets, since he was clearly unfamiliar with the concept. He did bring out, unprompted, various papers and insisted that I take away copies with me. These included a certificate relating to his father's trial at Nuremberg, which said that no proof of complicity in the Holocaust had been found (which is not quite the same as a declaration of innocence); a letter from his father's lawyer saying that he had heard that Otto Meissner Sr. had saved many people; and a letter from Pope Pius XII from 1953, regretting his father's death—though given that Pope's track record as Nuncio to Berlin during Hitler's rise to power, and his subsequent controversial concordats with the Nazi regime, he was perhaps a compromised referee.

Altogether, I found the dinner and interview with Hans-Otto Meissner one of the most unpleasant experiences of the whole trip. We never did get to film him as he was unwell a few weeks later and had to cancel; he died the following year.

* * *

Karen Liebreich

Hans Feld and Leni Riefenstahl

We interviewed only one Jewish film personality for the programme—unsurprisingly, as nearly all other Jews would have fled or been murdered. Hans Feld was born in 1902 into a liberal Prussian-Jewish family. He studied law, writing a doctorate on 'Ministerial responsibility as the basis of modern democracy.' In 1926, he joined the daily film newspaper, *Film-Kurier*, the voice of the industry, which aimed "to inform audiences about all trends in the field of cinematography, and to convert wider circles to this young art form... In addition, the *Film-Kurier* will serve as the main newspaper for the entire film industry, reporting on a daily basis about everything new that might be of interest to the professional."[57] After six months, he was taken on full time, with special responsibility for covering film prizes, and soon rose to be editor, by which time it was the undisputed leading film journal in Europe. There was so much material and it was so popular that there were often three daily editions, an astonishing fact

---

[57] 1 June 1919, quoted in Sabine Hake, *The Cinema's Third Machine: Writing on Film in Germany, 1907-1933* (University of Nebraska Press, 1993), p.115. Feld began writing for the magazine in 1926 (not 1921 as Hake says, when he was only nineteen and still at university), and became editor shortly thereafter.

which serves to underline the economic and cultural importance of the film industry in the 1930s.[58]

Feld had a very direct and spontaneous style of criticism, usually dictating his reviews straight into a Dictaphone for publication the day after the premiere. He also fought for union employment rights, protested against political censorship and attacked the domination of American film. He helped to draw the public's attention to exciting developments in Russian film, and set up a couple of subsidiary magazines, *Die Film-musik* and *Die Avantgarde*. He supported Edmund Meisel, the talented young composer who wrote the music for Eisenstein's *Battleship Potemkin* during a twelve-day burst of creativity, and was friends with leading film figures, such as Sergei Eisenstein, Leni Riefenstahl and Conrad Veidt; scriptwriter, librettist and film critic Béla Balázs; and scriptwriter Carl Mayer. In 1927, he gave journalist and historian Lotte Eisner (later mentor to Werner Herzog) her start in film, commissioning her to write for the *Film-Kurier*.

In an interview in 1990, Feld described how he had been supposed to have dinner with Leni Riefenstahl in 1930 when she received the news that Marlene Dietrich

---

[58] For more on the Film-Kurier, see Christelle Georgette Le Faucheur, *Defining Nazi Film: The Film Press and the German Cinematic Project, 1933-1945*, PhD dissertation (University of Texas at Austin, 2012), pp.61 *seqq.*

had been cast as Sternberg's *Blaue Engel*, a role that Riefenstahl had assumed was hers for the taking. He described how she was so upset she stopped cooking him goulash and cancelled dinner.[59]

In 1932, after differences with the editor-in-chief Ernst Jaeger, Feld left the *Film-Kurier* and went to work for Aafa-Film AG as a dramaturg and head of production. That was the year that, in February, Jaeger invited Riefenstahl to accompany him to listen to Hitler speaking at the Sportpalast, and where she first felt the Führer's force and was blown away: "It seemed as if the earth's surface were spreading out in front of me, like a hemisphere that suddenly splits apart in the middle, spewing out an enormous jet of water, so powerful that it touched the sky and shook the earth," she later recalled. "I felt quite paralyzed."[60]

Riefenstahl's new enthusiasm destroyed the friendship between her and Feld. "She was full of enthusiasm, she had to tell us something," Feld said. "She had met the leader of the Nazi party, Adolf Hitler, and he told her that he had always been an admirer of her films. She must have noticed that something was wrong as she finished her story because she hastened to say that she was

---

[59] Retold in Audrey Salkeld, *A Portrait of Leni Riefenstahl* (London: Random House, 1997).
[60] Quoted in Robert A.Rosenbaum, *Waking to Danger: Americans and Nazi Germany, 1933-41* (Santa Barbara: Praeger, 2010), p.4.

convinced that once he would come to power all these excesses would be swept away. My wife and I were rather perturbed and we found it a chilling experience. After that we withdrew [from the friendship]."

In January 1933, the Nazis came to power and on 14 March, the Ministry of Public Enlightenment and Propaganda was set up with Dr Joseph Goebbels at its head. On 28 March the leaders of the film industry, including Hans Feld, were summoned to a Bierabend in the Hotel Kaiserhof in Berlin.

Goebbels told the assembly which films he admired: Eisenstein's beautifully made *Battleship Potemkin* ("so well made that it could make a Bolshevist of anyone without a firm philosophical footing"[61]); the American *Anna Karenina*, starring Greta Garbo, which demonstrated the true art of film; Fritz Lang's modern version of the *Nibelungen* and Luis Trenker's *Der Rebell*, which dealt with the Tyrolean struggle for freedom. Goebbels saw a spiritual crisis in the film world which needed root and branch reform. From now on all films were to have their roots firmly embedded in the soil of national socialism. These were to set an example for the kind of new, ideologically conscious and politically engaged films that

---

[61] Quoted in Klaus Kreimeier, *The Ufa Story: A History of Germany's Greatest Film Company, 1918-1945* (University of California Press, 1999), p.209.

he expected from his film industry.[62] Hans Feld looked around as Goebbels harangued the film-makers. The room was surrounded by impassive Sturmtruppen, the Minister was by turns sneering, sarcastic and threatening. Only Feld and one other man refused to raise their arms in the Nazi salute. He knew what it meant.

The *Film-Kurier* had been Aryanised, with all Jews forced out. The editor, Jaeger, a Social Democrat with a Jewish wife, was hired by Riefenstahl as her press chief and later escaped to the United States while on a trip with her. The day before the Kaiserhof meeting, Goebbels had called for a boycott of all Jewish businesses. "The Jewish press whined with fear and dismay,"[63] he wrote. Within days of the Kaiserhof meeting, Feld and his wife fled to Prague, where he founded the monthly *Die Kritik,* aimed at creating bridges between Czech artists such as Max Brod and Karel Čapek. He scrabbled for work as a script editor, a cutter or a dialogue coach for German versions. He wrote two scripts and met Lida Baarova, later Goebbels' lover. But it was a hand-to-mouth existence, and prospects in Czechoslovakia looked increasingly bleak.

In 1935, Feld moved to London where he initially tried to continue his film critical writing and worked with John Grierson, Ivor Montagu and Alberto Cavalcanti. He

---

[62] http://www.filmportal.de/en/material/die-goebbels-rede-im-kaiserhof-am-2831933
[63] Kreimeier, *The Ufa Story,* p.209.

prepared a remake of D. W. Griffiths' *Orphans of the Storm*, but financial problems intervened, and from 1937, he worked in a food import company.

Feld talked us through scenes from Riefenstahl's *Triumph des Willens (Triumph of the Will)*, her film about the 1934 Nazi Party Congress in Nuremberg. We sat him in front of a Steenbeck film viewing table and played the film, while he analysed his old friend's techniques. Across the little screen, before the old man's eyes, marched the soldiers of the Reich, in perfect synchronicity, and even on the tiny square before him the power of the sounds and the images was clear. It was no wonder he and his wife had packed up their bags shortly after this film came out. He described its power: "I would say that it was choreographed, orchestrated like a symphony. There is a score marrying sound, music and vision. The rhythm of the march, the massed ranks, then you have got the solitary figure of the Leader. Whenever you see the outstretched arms, the Roman greeting, then you see the masses, and that is accompanied by passionate music. It's like a drug, the feeling, the emotion—because you can only be driven to a hero's death by emotion. The close-ups are a point of concentrated power. You see that Nazi in half-profile, [he represents] composed strength, and then you have got the swastika marching at you, grabbing at you, and you become part of it, and then you see your comrades: you are not alone. And there's always the father figure the Leader, [like] El Cid, Charlton Heston. And this is carefully prepared to be built up to a climax."

Riefenstahl's views are well known and have been much discussed. She always claimed to be just an innocent artist, interested only in the artistic integrity of her work. In our programme, she said: "[Hitler] was very natural, he spoke like a normal person to me, and only about my work so it was not difficult to speak with him. We have never spoken about things that I don't understand, only about things to do with my work, and naturally at this time he was for me a very important person and I was very proud that he had such confidence in me."[64]

Hitler's patronage allowed Riefenstahl to bypass the normal procedures and checks that Goebbels usually insisted on. As Hippler told us: "Riefenstahl angered Goebbels because she was given the opportunity to make films by Hitler personally. So Goebbels had no control over her whatsoever."

Feld's world, meanwhile, was shattered. One of the most knowledgeable and influential men in his field, he was exiled from his profession, his language and his homeland. Though he managed to create a life of reasonable comfort in London, he never recovered his place in the culture of his time.

---

[64] Interview originally filmed in 1972, used in *We Have Ways of Making you Think*.

Walter Frentz

I interviewed one of Riefenstahl's cameramen. Walter Frentz had been a cameraman specialising in kayaking films, before being recommended to Leni Riefenstahl by Albert Speer, with whom he used to go paddling,[65] to work on *Sieg des Glaubens (The Victory of Faith)*, a 1933 film about the Fifth Nazi party rally. For their next film together, *Triumph des Willens (Triumph of the Will)*. Riefenstahl developed the tracking shot, which had been tried earlier, but always on fixed rails. She explained her breakthrough in our programme: "I had only one idea. It was the first time it was done. I thought everything must be moving, and to do this was new. So I mentioned to my camera man that he should take roller skates. So they tried to do this with roller skates. Before this the newsreels were always still, not moving, or just a little bit of moving, but not really moving and this was new. And I feel the rhythm of this and this gives it life."

After the success of *Triumph*, Goebbels' Propaganda Ministry commissioned Frentz to create *Hände am Werk (Hands at Work – A Song of German Work)*, for which he was in charge of scenography and camerawork. For Frentz, the images, rather than the words, were important. He told me that propaganda in

---

[65] Gitta Sereny, *Albert Speer: His Battle with Truth* (London: Picador, 1996), p.129.

itself was dull, it was just a commission. The challenge was to try and make it interesting and visually effective.

Leni Riefenstahl again employed Frentz when she was commissioned to create a film celebrating the 1936 Olympics. Frentz was responsible for filming the sailing and the marathon. His innovative solution for one was to film the horizon and the water, making the viewer feel he was right *in medias res*. For the longueurs of the marathon, they decided to film the runners' feet from above from a lorry, slowing the pace to show how tired the participants were and making the sound louder and louder as they drew closer to the stadium. Both sports were filmed using innovative and successful solutions.

Either because of his work on *Olympia*, or because he was a fine strapping chap in uniform—at 1m94 (6'4") the tallest of three suggested cameramen—Frentz became Hitler's personal cameraman in autumn 1939. From then until the Führer's death, he shot all of Hitler's personal material. He had accompanied Hitler to Vienna in 1938 and later went with Ribbentrop to Moscow, carrying the Olympic flame. When Hitler was told about the fall of France on 17 June 1940, Frentz was warned just before the Führer got the news so that he could catch the moment of glee on camera when Hitler was told and slapped his thigh in joy. Apparently people used to go several times to the cinema to see Hitler's happiness at the conquest, and it became a very famous shot.

As well as working for the Führer, he was also sent on special missions, accompanying Himmler to the Eastern front where he filmed a massacre in Minsk. Only a couple of hours after filming the slaughter of the Russians, he happily took charming photos of Russian children. A few days later, he proudly noted that on his thirty-fourth birthday, he was allocated an honoured seat just to the right hand of the Führer.[66] He was sent to the siege of Sebastopol, where 50% of his crew were killed, and later to capture the construction of the V1 and V2 rockets. He filmed Hitler almost until the bitter end, although in the very last days, Hitler was trembling so much he was almost unfilmable.

When I interviewed him, Frentz lived with his painter wife in a lovely house overlooking Lake Constance in the pleasant spa town of Überlingen, yet another example of a German with close links to the Nazi regime who was living in luxury. Frentz argued that he never joined the Nazi party, he merely documented—he never produced, only reproduced.[67] After the war he was interned by the Americans for a few months before returning to work as lecturer on photography and then as a cameraman at the Helsinki Olympics of 1952. He was

---

[66]http://einestages.spiegel.de/static/topicalbumbackground/2735/das_auge_des_dritten_reiches.html
[67] Quoted in Frentz's obituary by David Childs in the *Independent*, 27 July 2004.

extremely charming, still handsome, very sporty and coherent.

After our initial discussions, he took me upstairs with some mystery. He bent and pulled out a heavy trunk filled with large colour photos of Hitler and his circle. Probably it was priceless. He asked me if I would like to buy it. I refused, revolted at the thought that anyone complicit in the regime should be making money from their dubious history. David Irving, controversial British historian, used them without scruples. After his death in 2004, his son brought out a spectacular colour tome. Now I rather regret my swift and moral decision. It would certainly have been worth a fortune, both financially and in historical terms.

After my visit, he decided that since I was dealing more with entertainment films, and he had worked in documentaries and personally for Hitler, he was not the right person for our film and refused to be filmed. Maybe my refusal to pay him lots of money for his Nazi images influenced his decision.

* * *

Arthur Maria Rabenalt

We interviewed the Austrian film director Arthur Maria Rabenalt at the Vier Jahreszeiten Kempinski Hotel in Munich. He was fat and wheezy, a sort of Teutonic Robert Morley. He had directed light comedies in Austria before going to Germany during the war, where he was responsible for such patriotic ham as the 1941 *Reitet für Deutschland* (*He rides for Germany*), based on a biography of a famous horseman who overcomes disability to win a surprise victory at the Geneva Steeplechase Competition. He later claimed it was "straightforwardly patriotic and ...made with no political intent"[68], but it was considered such successful propaganda that after the war the Americans banned him from working for two years, while the Russians deported the horse who starred in the film. After the war, he made many more forgettable films, shading into soft core porn.

He told us that Goebbels "was the greatest supporter of entertainment films as he was a film fan. He liked pretty women; basically he liked exactly what the public liked. The entertainment film had a political purpose. That political purpose was to get the audience

---

[68] Arthur Maria Rabenalt, *Film im Zwielicht: Uber den unpolitischen Film des Dritten Reiches und die Begrenzung des totalitären Anspruches* (Munich: Copress-Verlag, 1958).

off the streets, away from their household cares and family worries." For Rabenalt, Goebbels' film policy was strictly escapist, his directors were there to provide a few hours of relief for the war weary. For *Münchhausen*, for instance, Hans Albers' Baron travelled in glorious Agfacolor to Turkish harems, famously flew on a cannonball, visited the moon in a hot air balloon and had many other amusing adventures. The film was released one month after Goebbels' Total War speech, as the Germans were coming to terms with their defeat by the Soviet army. As Rabenalt said about *Münchhausen*: "Towns were burning, but the people were queuing in the streets so that they could watch films about a fashionable and elegant world."

He had been curious as to why actresses would sleep with Goebbels, who was no Adonis, apart from their obvious desire to get a bigger role in the next film. Rabenalt told us how he had interrogated some of his female stars: "There were women to whom I said 'What? You had a date?' And they said, 'Yes, it was interesting. I wanted to get to know a man of world history. You don't miss an opportunity like that.'"

* * *

Norbert Schultze

My favourite Nazi interviewee was Norbert Schultze, who achieved worldwide fame by writing the music for the song 'Lili Marlene.' He was a very spry and tanned elderly gentleman, white-haired, very sharp, eighty years old but seeming much younger, wearing a denim jacket. He lived most of the year in Majorca with his third wife, which accounted for his tan. He wrote the music for many of the Nazi film hits of the time, including *Feuertaufe (Baptism of Fire)*, *Bismarck, Kolberg* and *Ich klage an (I accuse)*.

Ever since the introduction of the first sound film to Germany, Al Jolson's *Singing Fool*, which premiered in Berlin in 1929—and arguably even earlier as pianists accompanied silent films with extempore scores—the importance of music in film had been acknowledged. After seeing the film, Goebbels wrote in his diary, "I was surprised about the already far advanced technology of sound film. Here is the future."

In 1939, Wolfgang Liebeneiner, soon to be appointed head of production at Ufa (1942 – 1945), wrote an essay on the importance of music in film. According to him, Germany was the country "that created music and conquered the world with it," and now it could be harnessed to enhance and emphasise the rhythm of films.

In the words of one historian, "As conceived by Nazi theorists, film music proved essential to set collective moods and bond the people, to mobilize desire and regenerate lost experiences of community."[69]

We interviewed Schultze in the Hansa Sound Studios in Kreuzberg, where Iggy Pop, David Bowie and Nick Cave had recorded some of their most famous hits. He sat at a grand piano in the Meistersaal recording hall, with its famously wonderful acoustics, and used the grand piano to illustrate his points. He played us the beautiful song 'Lili Marlene' which, even when sung in his elderly voice, was still moving. He wrote the music to the 1915 poem in 1938, and it was first broadcast as sung by Lale Anderson, without his prior knowledge, in 1941. This was one of the best interviews I ever conducted.

He told me that Goebbels saw himself as "a cultural Pope"; he knew about theatre, film and music, and he loved playing the role of the great patron and connoisseur. Schultze considered Goebbels easily the most intelligent of the Nazi leaders, but he compared him to Satan. Goebbels must have known it was all over years before the end. "He used Hitler to create his own Reich, to make up for the big chip on his shoulder."

---

[69] Lutz Koepnick, *The Dark Mirror: German Cinema Between Hitler and Hollywood* (Berkeley: University of California Press, 2002), p.42.

He described Goebbels' hands-on approach to all aspects of film-making, including the music. He was asked to prepare a song to inspire the troops for Operation Barbarossa, the invasion of Russia, called *Von Finnland bis zum Schwarzen Meer (From Finland to the Black Sea)*. "And then we drove out to Lanke to play it to the Minister. At first I thought, what might he have to say about it, he doesn't know anything about music. I was in for a surprise. I went in and he sat down next to me on the piano bench. He looked at my music sheets and said, 'Let me have a go'. I had to slide along the bench and he sat next to me and he played. He said, 'I don't like this bit… It's too old-fashioned, why don't you do it like this…' And I said, 'You're absolutely right, Herr Minister. It is better.' In propaganda terms the shorter version was more effective."

Schultze played us one of his wartime hits—less popular outside the Third Reich for obvious reasons—which was called *Bomben auf Engelland (Bombs on England)*, the theme for the film *Feuertaufe (Baptism of Fire)*. This had been initiated by Göring, not Goebbels, and had initially been made for the German Air Ministry, but Hitler thought it was marvellous, so it was decided to issue it on general release. Important Danes and Norwegians were invited to a private screening on 5 April 1940 at the German Embassy in Oslo to prepare them for what was about to happen to their countries a few days later.

In fact, when Schultze saw *Feuertaufe*, with its long scene of flying over Warsaw, showing the houses all bombed out, he was shocked. "I found it terrible, so I wrote a mourning march. The Air Ministry officials were there for the screening and they watched. There was an orchestra and the conductor was following the film on the screen. The officials said stop, and sent the orchestra out. This is terrible, they cried, we feel real sympathy for the enemy. I said, yes, this is a terrible scene so I wrote sad music for it. Then the director suggested that we added commentary, saying, "And all this destruction is your fault Mr Chamberlain," over the music. And this was accepted. I also added Polish songs, but again they laid a text over it."

However, the film needed a new ending before release because by then the enemy was Britain, and it also needed a new theme tune, one that would emphasise the romance of the pilots. "This is what happens when the German Luftwaffe strikes," intoned the commentary. "It will also know how to strike at the guiltiest of the guilty."

"Now our new enemy was England," explained Schultze, "and there had to be an incredible pilot song at the end, 'The battle against England.' I wrote the music, and unfortunately the audience loved it. It was a hit tune, well anyhow it was more of a hit than a march." He played it for us:

Our newest weapon has been baptised and tempered in the flames.
Now the winged host reaches out to the sea.
We are ready for battle.
Forward against the British Lion for the last decisive blow.
We sit in judgement. A world empire collapses. That'll be our proudest day.
Comrade, comrade - all the girls must wait.
Comrade comrade - the order is given, we are off.
Comrade, comrade, the solution is clear.
Attack the enemy! Attack the enemy!
Bombs on England!

"That was it—bombs on England," he repeated with a rueful smile. "I didn't think anything of it at the time. Later I was asked, 'How could you—an educated person—inflict bombs on England, on a cultured nation.' I replied, 'Well, good God, where else should our pilots drop their bombs?' They were our enemy, so of course on England. That's how naive I was!"

Goebbels thought *Bomben auf Engelland* was too melodramatic and operetta-ish, too much like a frothier film, *Rosen in Tirol*. He said, "It's like *What does little Billy think of war* ("Wie sich der kleine Moritz Krieg vorstellt?")" but it was a huge hit." It was often used as a soundtrack to accompany the *Wochenschau*, the weekly news films. However, Schultze was never invited to meet Hitler and, he told me with a twinkle that he had felt very offended by the omission at the time.

When I asked Schultze about propaganda techniques, he told me that in 1934 he had done an advert for Nivea. "I asked them whether their product was so much better," he told me. "On the contrary, they replied, it was worse because they used cheaper products, but this meant they could spend more money on advertising." He shrugged his shoulders: "But one does the job, there are lots of lies in the world." As for *Bomben auf Engelland*, Schultze said, "I did it to help my country, not to help the Nazis."

The final scene of *Feuertaufe* used Schultze's catchy hit tune again as the Luftwaffe appeared, using trick photography, to dive-bomb the British Isles. "The song *Bomben auf Engelland* was enthusiastically received," noted the customary scrupulous secret police report on audience reaction.[70]

The conversation turned to *Kolberg*. The Propaganda Ministry decided exactly who should play what, and who should do the music. Schultze was not keen as the film consisted primarily of battles. "I wanted to do something like *Immensee*," he said sadly. Subtitled *Ein deutsches Volkslied (A German Folksong)*, *Immensee* (1943) was

---

[70] Bundesarchiv Koblenz R58/184, 08-10 vol 145.1940, cited by Lutz Becker.

also directed by Harlan and starred Kristina Söderbaum. It told the story of a woman remaining faithful to her husband, even after his death—and her Heimat, in spite of the claims of her childhood love. It was clearly aimed at reassuring soldiers at the front that their wives remained faithful. Unfortunately for Schultze, another composer won that contract.

There was no choice. *Kolberg* was obviously an important film, so crucial that Goebbels diverted many soldiers from the war effort to take part as extras. Schultze told us how Harlan gathered the cast together in the marketplace and made a big speech: "You are lucky enough to be allowed to take part in an absolutely crucial moment in the German nation's history. This film is vital for the future of the Volk. So if necessary you will stand still for the whole night and not move and behave. And then there will be a big bowl of pea soup." He was so convincing that Schultze said to himself, "I must make a big effort too." And he wrote the music to *Das Volk steht auf, der Sturm bricht los* (*People arise, the storm is coming*), re-using the closing evocation from Goebbels' Total War speech of 1943 in the unlikely event that anyone might have missed the parallels, a rousing march that, in the film version at least, brought the entire population out onto the streets in defence of the town.

"Goebbels was of course very enthusiastic about the performance of the artists in such a film because he said the film *Kolberg* will survive us all. Dreadful, dreadful!" He shook his head sadly.

He recalled how impressive he had found the scenes where the burghers are all digging, throwing up fortifications around the town, and it inspired him to create heroic music. He also found Söderbaum very impressive, mainly, he said, "Because she was able to weave and act at the same time."

Kolberg was considered so important that they parachuted a copy of the film into the beleaguered town of La Rochelle for the premiere. It showed the French as the enemies, raping and pillaging. Söderbaum's character is attacked, but she escapes, and the town is saved. During the last scenes on the beach, Nettelbeck, the local patriot who has rallied the citizen army to defend its town, says to her: "You gave everything you had Maria, but it wasn't in vain. Death and victory are intertwined. That's normal. Greatness is always born only out of pain."

Schultze found the film one-sided (which is an amusing thought, considering its propaganda aims) and told me that he refused to do the music for a rape scene. Schultze said, "Harlan was unscrupulous. He would do anything to make the film; he didn't care about the effect."[71]

---

[71] He said he complained to Harlan about the rape, so that scene has no music. It must have been cut completely from the final version.

Schultze admitted that he would have done the music for *Jud Süß* had he been asked. He found it a silly question, saying that knowing what he did then in the same situation he would act exactly the same way. He spoke to a friend in Prague in 1944 who told him that he was sending his young 17-year-old soldiers to their deaths, but asked "What can I do?" If he tells them it's hopeless, they'll die miserable; if they refuse to fight, they'll be shot; if he doesn't order them, he'll be shot, and someone else will order them. It's an impossible choice. So he tries to encourage them to fight with bravado and to die feeling that it was a worthwhile sacrifice. A week after this conversation, Schultze read that his friend had died in battle. He was very moved by this conversation.

After the programme was done, we communicated for some time. He had written an opera "for small and large people" called *Schwarzer Peter*. This was based on a children's card game, a bit like Happy Families, with the eponymous Black Peter, a lucky chimney sweep, as the lead character, and I had the idea to bring a production over to London. Sadly, it came to nothing.

* * *

Karen Liebreich

Kristina Söderbaum

We drove to Horw, near Lucerne, to interview Kristina Söderbaum, star of many films, most of them directed by her husband, Veit Harlan, including the notoriously anti-Semitic *Jud Süß* and the ridiculous epic, *Kolberg*. She was so often drowned in her films (and occasionally raped) that she became known as the Reichswasserleiche, the official State Water Corpse. Throughout her career, her "impulsiveness and naiveté... were depicted as erotic qualities and her downfall often took shape as a process of sexual defilement, inviting audiences to derive a kind of sadistic pleasure from the character's vulnerability and loss of innocence... a compelling image of victimhood and surrender."[72]

The interview took place at the house of her protector, Edie Bechter. Bechter conducted all the preparatory discussions with me. He pretended to be very sad about the treatment of the Jews and told me he wished to set up a fund to donate money to impoverished Jews in Israel. Would I help him to set up such a fund? Of course, I replied. Would I act as a sort of trustee to find deserving recipients of such funds? Of course. Given

---

[72] Jana Francesca Bruns, *Nazi Cinema's New Women* (Cambridge: Cambridge University Press, 2009), p.13.

these assurances, he would facilitate the interview with Söderbaum. Presumably, he thought I would give her an easier ride if I was hoping for lots of donations afterwards. Once the interview was done, Mr Bechter evaporated, and I never heard from him again. I can't say that it changed the way I interviewed her, though I was naive enough at the time to think the old Nazi genuine in his offer. But he was naive to think that his offers to fund Jewish orphanages would influence our programme.

During my preliminary interview, Mr Bechter answered questions on behalf of the star. "No, of course, Kristina would have hung herself if she'd known the problems *Jud Süß* would bring." Bechter had been her number one fan and then best friend and was now in a very strange relationship with her. He wore her husband's wedding ring, and his house was full of fan mementos, such as photos of Kristina. He kept two spectacular piebald Great Danes because her character in *Opfergang* had kept Great Danes and he had Veit Harlan's work chair and his death mask. He said he had been the chief defender during Harlan's trial after the war, although I have been unable to find any reference to him in any of the books about Harlan, including Harlan's autobiography.

Kristina Söderbaum, even at the age of eighty, was still very beautiful in a traditional pink and white baby doll style. She had been one of the greatest stars of her era, and even in the 1950s, polls still showed her to be the second-most popular film actress with the German public.[73] Swedish by birth, she had big greeny-blue eyes, white curly hair, blue eyeliner, blue eyelashes and bright pink lipstick. A promotional leaflet from Ufa in 1942 described her as "the biggest natural talent in German film these days... Her acting lessons mainly consisted of refining her German pronunciation."[74] In a two-page questionnaire she filled in in 1935, she described herself as 100% Aryan (75% Swedish, 22% Danish, 3% Russian = 100% Aryan).[75] She told me she had had bad experiences with the media, so she never gave interviews now. She had a lovely smile.

She seemed to me to be a very sweet, vague old lady, who had been totally under the influence of her husband. Harlan was one of the Nazis' top film directors and the only director from the Nazi era to be charged with war crimes. He had been married to a Jewish woman from 1922 to 1924 (who died in Auschwitz in 1943), then to Hilde Körber, an Austrian actress who was already in labour with their first child at their wedding in 1929. She claimed to have been sexually assaulted by Fritz Kortner, a well-known Jewish actor who was then portrayed in the

---

[73] Randall Halle, Margaret McCarthy (eds.), *Light Motives: German Popular Film in Perspective*, (Detroit: Wayne State University Press, 2003), p.111.
[74] Quoted in Antje Ascheid, *Hitler's Heroines: Stardom and Womanhood in Nazi Cinema* (Philadelphia: Temple University Press, 2003), p.42.
[75] Bruns, *Nazi Cinema's New Women,* p.177.

Nazi press as a rampant Jewish rapist, with Harlan threatening to horse-whip him. Kortner fled into exile and became a close associate of Bertolt Brecht and Peter Lorre. In a further twist, Hilde Körber was best friend to Lida Baarova, the Czech actress with whom Joseph Goebbels had become infatuated in late 1935, and helped them to arrange love trysts at her house. Söderbaum said that Goebbels wished Harlan to divorce his wife so that he, Harlan, could marry Baarova to get German nationality. Having Slav papers was unhelpful for the Czech actress. Instead, in 1939, Harlan married Söderbaum, and Hitler put a stop to Goebbels' plans to run away with Baarova. Although it may have cast a temporary *froideur* on the relationship between the Minister and his top film director, it failed to have any lasting effect; Harlan continued his career as one of the most successful directors of the time, becoming Goebbels' "go to" person for films of special importance, such as *Jud Suß* and *Kolberg*.

Söderbaum claimed that Goebbels didn't much like her, partially explained by her role in the Baarova affair. Perhaps he also found her insipid and too blonde, as his taste—apart from his wife Magda—generally ran to dark-haired actresses. "He told me I was not sexy but erotic." In spite of that, she said, "Terribly many people fell in love with me. But whether that made me a sex symbol or not, I don't know." For her part, she found that

"Goebbels had very nice eyes, but," she added with a laugh, "He was a devil!"

She said that Hitler, on the other hand, was always very pleasant to her, for instance when they met in the Artists' Club and her husband always remarked on Hitler's amazing eyes. She told me she was not unimpressed by his eyes.

At this the minder intervened to say he had a list of actresses who had slept with Goebbels. Unfortunately, he refused to show it to me. Söderbaum interrupted to say that Margot Hielscher had definitely slept with Goebbels and had been rewarded with a role in *Das Herz der Königin*, as one of Mary Queen of Scots' handmaidens, and that she had been well known as Goebbels' brief mistress. She was supposed to be in Harlan's 1944 film, *Opfergang*, but by then she had fallen from favour, and Söderbaum got the starring role instead.

Söderbaum could be described as the archetypical feminists' nightmare. A beautiful woman, a nice lady, a very convincing actress, totally obedient and devoted to her forceful husband, Söderbaum was not allowed to act in any but her husband's films. She described herself to me as living "in a gilded cage,"—"I went everywhere in a limo"—but I saw no signs of curiosity in her about the life beyond the bars, or that she might even wish to stretch her wings. In her autobiography, she seemed surprised by the post-war reaction, the hostility towards Harlan, astonished, for instance, that her children were taunted as Nazis at school in Sweden.[76]

Goebbels was hugely powerful, she said, and could—and did—intervene in every aspect of a film, including script and casting. She told me how he changed the ending of the very successful *Die goldene Stadt (The Golden Town)* of 1942, the second ever German colour film. It made some a fortune at the box office.[77] Söderbaum's character, Anna, wants to leave her rural home and strict father and go to Prague, the Golden City of the title, the home city of her Czech mother. Eventually she runs away, gets pregnant in the city, returns to the country and kills herself, just like her mother did, in a nasty swamp. The final scene shows the swamp, which has been converted into fertile cornfields by the heroic lover who stayed behind. According to Söderbaum, the director, Harlan, had finished the film with a happy ending for the lovers: the father dead, the Czech seducer returned to the farm with Anna, the lovers reunited. Then Goebbels changed the ending, which she said she didn't even know at the time, and they threw a dummy into the marsh, killing off her character in a tragic ending. People must be encouraged to stay "*auf's Land*", on the farm. Rural life

---

[76] Kristina Söderbaum, *Nichts bleibt immer so: Rückblenden auf ein Leben vor und hinter der Kamera* (Bayreuth: Hestia, 1984).
[77] *Light Motives*, p.111, claims it made 43 million Reichsmark, though that seems very high.

represented racial hygiene; *Blut und Boden*—Blood and Soil—must win over the decadent city, and sleeping around with nasty Slavs who are poisoning pure Aryan blood lines leads only to tragedy. Perhaps there was a hint of sour grapes from the Minister, who had been forced to give up his own Slav girlfriend, though, of course, things are different for unfaithful men. Goebbels wrote of being moved by the "erotics of death"[78] as Söderbaum played the State Water Corpse once more. In her memoirs, she later bemoaned her fate, always having to play "despondent women who ended up invariably in the sea or the swamp"[79] instead of being allowed to star in a jolly comedy.

Söderbaum told me that when they were in Venice to receive a prize for *Die goldene Stadt* (she won the Volpi Cup for best actress) and she was to film a scene where she had to jump naked from a gondola, Goebbels dared her and said she wouldn't do it, so she took off her dress, kept her petticoat on and jumped in. It had caused a huge scandal at the time, and she was very keen to underline to me that she had kept her petticoat on!

Goebbels insisted that Harlan, whom she claimed was reluctant to be involved in the film, direct *Jud Süß* and that she star. The story starts in 1733 with the coronation of the Duke of Württemberg. The moneylender Joseph

---

[78] *Light Motives*, p.115.
[79] Bruns, *Nazi Cinema's New Women*, p.178.

Oppenheimer Süß inveigles his way into the duke's graces The brochure the film company issued at the time explains the story. "Clean-shaven and dressed like a gentleman the Jew Süss Oppenheimer contrives to be appointed Finance Minister to the Duke of Württemberg... The Jew Süss Oppenheimer violates the beautiful Dorothea Sturm, an outrageous act which confirms the extent of his guilt... Jew, hands off German women!"[80] The Nuremberg laws had outlawed sexual relations between Jews and non-Jews in 1935, but assimilated Jews who tried to 'dress like gentlemen' were considered particularly dangerous for German women. Süß's character Dorothea is indeed tempted by the charismatic financier's seduction techniques. After her violation, in accordance with Söderbaum's customary fate, she drowns herself and Süß, gibbering for mercy, is punished with a public execution. In the film, all Jews who under his influence had been permitted entry to the town, were immediately banished from Stuttgart. The film summarises: "May posterity honour this law so that much suffering to their property, life, and the blood of their children and their children's children might be spared them."[81]

In his post-war memoirs, an apologia for his outstanding career under the Nazis, Veit Harlan claimed that he had tried to avoid any involvement in *Jud Süß* until

---

[80] From a leaflet issued by Terra-Filmkunst.
[81] Rentschler, *Ministry of Illusion,* p. 152.

warned that this would result in his being shot as a deserter. Söderbaum claimed he tried to volunteer for the front rather than direct.[82] Arthur Maria Rabenalt, whom we interviewed later, denied this, saying that Harlan was very keen to direct the film. At any rate, it was a great success at the German box office, and Harlan was able to demand an extra RM100,000 for future productions. The film department agreed, as long as "there are similar performances to those portrayed in *Jud Süß*."[83]

Söderbaum was the obvious casting for the role. As she told us: "They wanted me, this blonde, not very intelligent, nice, Aryan girl." At least she was aware of her image—a sort of infantilised and fluffy pretty girl, often either at the mercy of a rapacious man, or needing guidance from a strong masculine hand to set her on the right path. The issue might be marital fidelity faced with an absent husband away at the Front, love of the Fatherland, the importance of the rural Heimat, self-sacrifice in the face of overwhelming odds, but the gentle blonde was always obedient and willing.

Söderbaum told me that *Jud Süß* was not an anti-Semitic film. On the contrary, she said, everyone felt sympathetic towards the title character. Her opinion does leave open the question of why Himmler would order that

---

[82] Söderbaum, *Nichts bleibt immer so,* p.148.
[83] Jo Fox, *Filming Women in the Third Reich* (Oxford & New York: Berg, 2000), p.169.

the film be shown to all SS units and to concentration camp guards[84] on the grounds that it put them in the right frame of mind for the work they were to do. Ferdinand Marian played Süß, "the Jew in disguise". When he protested that he would ruin his fan base playing such an unsympathetic character, Goebbels pointed out that he had recently played Iago to great acclaim. "But that was Shakespeare," he cried. "And I," shouted the minister, putting his face close to Marian's, "I am Joseph Goebbels!"[85] In 1946, either drunk with relief at having been permitted to act once more now that the Nazis had been defeated, according to one version, or—according to another—deliberately committing suicide because he was overwhelmed with guilt at his role in *Jud Süß,* Marian died in a car crash.[86] Werner Krauss played all the other Jewish roles in the film in order, as Harlan explained, to show that "the pious Patriarch, the wily swindler, the penny-pinching merchant and so on are ultimately derived from the same roots."[87]

A report on audience reaction to the film by the Strasburg Security Police noted that "the film presents a

---

[84] Himmler's order of 30 September 1940; See Goebbels diary, 9 November 1939; 5, 15 and 18 December 1939; 18 January 1940; 2 February 1940; 8 March 1941.
[85] Story told by Söderbaum, *Nichts bleibt immer so,* pp. 149-150.
[86] David Stewart Hull, *Film in the Third Reich: A study of the German cinema, 1933-45* (University of California Press, 1969), p.269.
[87] Veit Harlan in *Der Film,* 20 January 1940, quoted in Erwin Leiser, *Nazi Cinema* (London: Macmillan, 1974), p.152.

once and for all picture of the 'Wandering Jew' and his parasitic existence as the essence of evil.... The film's effect is correspondingly powerful. The events on the screen are so realistic that audiences are constantly provoked to comment and shouting [...] 'Dirty pig Jew!', 'You Jewish swine!', 'Filthy Jew boy!' are comments often heard, particularly from women; and the rape scene, linked as it is with the only just bearable torture scene, really outrages people.... There is only one verdict: *Jud Süß* is *the* best film in a long time."[88] By 1943, 20.3million viewers throughout Europe had seen it. After the premiere, Goebbels wrote in his diary on 25 September 1940, "A very large audience with almost the entire Reich Cabinet. The film is an incredible success. One hears only enthusiastic responses. The whole room raves. That's exactly what I had hoped for." Apparently the film continued to be used after the war as anti-Israeli propaganda.[89]

When I asked Söderbaum why she went along with *Jud Süß*, she said she had had no choice. I asked why she had not pretended to have a sore throat like Marianne Hoppe, and she said, "I was ill, I had just given birth and was breastfeeding." She said we couldn't do it badly, "because Veit wanted to do everything well." In her autobiography, she told how she claimed to be ill, but

---

[88] Special Squad II/1, quoted in Leiser, *Nazi Cinema*, p.153. Bruns, *Nazi Cinema's New Women*, p.214.
[89] Rentschler, *Ministry of Illusion*, pp.149-150.

Goebbels pointed out that she had already made herself available for other roles.[90]

Söderbaum said that Harlan got lots of Polish Jews to sing songs in the film, but Goebbels cut them because he felt they made the Jews seem sympathetic. She claimed that the final scenes were shot by Wolfgang Liebeneiner, director of the Ufa film studios, not by Harlan who "had many Jewish friends". But Harlan certainly filmed the scene in which the Jew brutally raped her, and which had such a dramatic effect on Nazi audiences. When we asked her about this scene, Söderbaum said: "When one looks at it today, it looks very different from then. Today we know so much more about the war, then we didn't know anything. Now we know it from the films we have seen, from terrible pictures of concentration camps and suchlike. Then suddenly it becomes much worse, and one says, 'For heaven's sake I helped with this!' When one acted in it—or even was forced to act in it—we didn't think like that. We didn't know what it would be used for." Although ignorance is a poor defence, it is hard to give the same benefit of the doubt to her husband.

Harlan was indicted in 1948, accused of crimes against humanity for directing an inflammatory film which slandered Jewry and therefore provoked pogroms. On 22

---

[90] Kristina Söderbaum, *Nichts bleibt immer so*, p.148.

July 1948, Harlan wrote to Rabbi Dr Joachim Prinz, vice-chair of the World Jewish Congress, claiming that the film was not anti-Semitic and had done little harm. Anyhow, he had been forced into it: "I will not talk in this letter of the pressures which were exerted on all artists. I would assure you, however, that I had nothing whatsoever to do with the Party, with anti-Semitism, or with the whole National Socialist ideology."

"However [my] trial ends," he wrote with a stunning lack of insight, "I am deeply convinced that it will bring harm to the Jews, harm to the defeated German Volk."

The Rabbi must have picked himself up off the floor at Harlan's suggestion that the harm caused to the Jews by discussing the matter could be in any way equivalent to the harm caused by the gas chambers. He responded very firmly: "Why Veit Harlan—as a person, as an artist, as a man, should be more important than the many thousands of men, women, and children who were dragged to their deaths by SS men who had been deeply impressed and deeply persuaded by your film—is beyond my comprehension. I have talked to people who saw with their own eyes, in Cracow in 1945 for instance, what effect your film had, and who later had to suffer for it themselves. Even perverted art can be perfect."

The rabbi went on to say: "And if—as I am told—your film is an artistic experience, then with all the resources of your great art it has succeeded in showing people through 'historical example'(what actual historical sources the film is based on in is another question) that a Jew's sole desires are power, avarice, desecration and a deep-rooted meanness... As for the misfortune the Jewish people may incur from the trial—let us worry about that. We have many worries. We can shoulder another one. This letter is a serious attempt to say to you that it would be better for you, aware of your own guilt, to await the outcome of the trial with dignity and composure."[91]

Harlan was, however, acquitted as it could not be proved that his film had actually led directly to the deaths of any Jews. "My party is art," he claimed. "I am a patriot. I love my homeland... I'm no politician. I'm a director."[92] After a few years he returned to directing, but he always claimed, self-pityingly, that his wartime films overshadowed his reputation. Nevertheless, he made nine feature films during the 1950s. Recent historians argue that Harlan and Söderbaum were the "casualties of an anti-fascist crusade initiated by vindictive leftist critics

---

[91]http://www.zeit.de/1949/10/der-jud-suess-film-und-die-menschlichkeit. Also quoted in Leiser, *Nazi Cinema*, pp. 155-156.
[92] Rentschler, *Ministry of Illusion*, p.166.

seeking to lock them up in history's poison cabinet along with other demons of the National Socialist past."[93]

As for Söderbaum, in her autobiography she wrote that *Jud Süß*, "Burnt a wound in my soul, and whenever it seems nearly healed over, it is ripped open once more. I know it will never heal. That is my fate, I must live with it."[94]

Söderbaum claimed that *Jud Süß* and *Kolberg* were "man's films", and told me she much preferred "typical" films such as *Opfergang, Immensee* and *Reise nach Tilsit*. Modern film historians agree with her verdict, calling *Kolberg* "a film by men, about men, and about war and the doctrines of war. Women just do not matter."[95] The star preferred more romantic fare; her favourite scene of all was in *Opfergang*, in the stable, where she says, "Wir lieben uns, und das wird schlimm." ("We're in love and that's bad news"). It was in this film that she galloped bareback along a beach in her underwear, representing unbridled sexuality and luring her lover, someone else's husband, from his marital duty. However, the wife was heroic and self-sacrificing, and it all paid off as the husband

---

[93] Bruns, *Nazi Cinema's New Women,* p.174, discussing the work of Norbert Grob and Frank Noack.
[94] Söderbaum, *Nichts bleibt immer so*, p.153.
[95] "Ganz Feuer und Flamme," John Whiteclay Chambers II & David Culbert, *World War II, Film, and History* (Oxford University Press, 1997), pp.69-70.

eventually abandoned Söderbaum and cleaved to his faithful wife in the final scenes.

She admitted that the actors were delighted to take part in *Kolberg*, since it meant they didn't have to go to the front. At first, Harlan was reluctant to take on the film, but then became very keen ("all fire and flame" according to Goebbels' diary).[96] Goebbels continually expressed his worries that Harlan was making "more of a Söderbaum film than a Nettelbeck film."[97] Nettelbeck was the heroic defender who begs Count von Gneisenau not to give up but to fight to the bitter end. Harlan wrote in his memoirs that "Goebbels saw himself as the character of Nettelbeck. He wanted to make Nettelbeck the great hero, to the detriment of Gneisenau."[98] For the filmmakers, the shelling of Kolberg during the Franco-Prussian war of 1806-7 represented the contemporary bombing of Hamburg, Dresden and Berlin; it extolled the idea of collective suicide through a kind of perverse obstinacy unto death. The unremitting message is that dying in war is a blessing.

Von Oven remembered his boss talking about *Kolberg*: "Goebbels even said to me that it was more important that the soldiers act in this film as extras rather

---

[96] 7 May 1943.
[97] 5 June 1943; 6 June 1943.
[98] Quoted in Fox, *Filming Women,* p.108.

than fight at the front which was no longer worth doing since we were in the midst of total collapse."

Söderbaum herself had to do a lot of pumping during the filming, which she found a bore. She remembered that the soldiers wore bandeaux made of toilet paper, such were the shortages. "I found it ridiculous to be filming when the enemy was coming nearer and nearer. One knew about the war and everything that was happening. Then to stand in front of the camera, I felt like an idiot."

I asked her if she regretted her part in the activities of the regime. She replied that it was 'like Tosca'. Feeling ignorant, as I was unfamiliar with Tosca, I didn't follow up the question, which I bitterly regretted when we went through the rushes. When the director asked me what she meant, I had absolutely no idea. Perhaps she thought of herself as an innocent following her lover to her doom.

On 19th March 1945, the real town of Kolberg (now Kolobrzeg on the Baltic coast of Poland) fell to the Allies. "We could do without this," wrote Goebbels in his diary on that day, in a comment that is breathtaking in its lack of realistic perspective. The imaginary war on the film set had become more real than the reality. Six weeks later, Hitler and Goebbels were dead.

Conclusion

We returned from our filming trip. Laurence Rees made a wonderful, award-winning documentary using the interviews, along with film extracts, clips from newsreel and an intelligent commentary that wove the story together and brought fresh insight to Goebbels' use of film for propaganda. The reviewers thought the programme was excellent and the archive footage fabulous.[99] Several papers complained that the interviews with the ageing Nazis were too apolitical and that they were allowed to get away with saying they were only obeying orders.[100] Rees went on to direct several more series about the Nazis, creating an invaluable archive of interviews with the men who had defined German history in such a dramatic and terrible way.

The people we interviewed are all dead now. Historians continue to study the films and film-makers of the period, and perhaps there may be a snippet of value in some of these interviews from my old notebooks.

---

[99] "Chilling, gripping" (*Daily Telegraph*), "Intriguing" (*Independent on Sunday*), "Distinguished" (*Sunday Times*), "highly entertaining" (*Sunday Telegraph*), "a cracker...terrific" (*Daily Mail*), "first-rate, superb" (*Times*).
[100] *Time Out, Times.*

List of films mentioned

Aus den Wolken kommt das Glück (Amphitryon), 1935
The most successful film of the year, directed by the half-Jewish Reinhold Schünzel, who emigrated to the USA in 1937.

Barcarole, 1934
Directed by Gerhard Lamprecht. Starring Lida Baarova, Gustav Fröhlich, Willy Birgel. Baarova moved in with Gustav Fröhlich, who had divorced his Jewish wife, and they set up home in Schwanenwerder, very near to Goebbels' Lanke villa.

Bismarck, 1940
Directed by Wolfgang Liebeneiner, this was – along with films about Frederick the Great – one of the 'great men' films that pleased Hitler so much. Germany was to be united, not by wishy washy liberal democracy as revealed during the arguments and intrigues of democracy, the dreams of 'a nation of poets and thinkers', but rather by Prussian Prime Minister Bismarck's duty to 'iron and blood' which would restore greater Germany.

Blaue Engel (The Blue Angel), 1930
Directed by Josef Sternberg, starring Marlene Dietrich, Emil Jannings, Kurt Gerron. A stylish classic, it brought Dietrich, with her song 'Falling in Love Again,' to international attention. Dietrich and Sternberg left Germany soon after. *The Blue Angel* was banned in Germany in 1933.

Capriolen, 1937
Directed by Gustaf Gründgens, starring Gründgens and Marianne Hoppe. Witty comedy about the relationship between a pilot and a journalist.

Effi Briest, see *Der Schritt vom Wege*

Es war eine rauschende Ballnacht
(*It was a Lovely Night at the Ball*), 1939
Directed by Carl Froehlich, starring Zarah Leander, Hans Stüwe, Marikka Rökk. A doomed love affair between Tchaikovsky and an aristocrat, sacrifices, deathbed declarations and sublime music.

Der Ewige Jud (The Eternal Jew), 1940
Directed by Fritz Hippler. Script by Eberhard Taubert, music by Franz Friedl. According to the opening credits it was "A film contribution to the problem of world Jewry." A supposed documentary film that became notorious as the most stridently anti-Semitic film produced during the Nazi period.

Feuertaufe (Baptism of Fire), 1940
Directed by Hans Bertram, a former air ace. Made for the German Air Ministry, the film glorified the destructive abilities of aerial bombing and featured an epilogue by Hermann Göring. After the German minorities in Poland suffer persecution, Poland attacks Germany and the German air force defends the country against aggression. The music by Norbert Schultze played an important role as the narration alternated with heroic song, and the catchy refrain, 'Bombs on England' provided a hummable ear-worm for audiences to take home from the cinema. Although "young people in particular have become very enthusiastic about the Luftwaffe as a result of this film... one section of the audience wanted even more action with live war scenes, others especially women, expressed sympathy for the Poles, and faced with the sight of Warsaw in ruins, the feeling was one of depression and anxiety about the 'horrors of war', rather than one of heroic pride."[101]

Die goldene Stadt (The Golden Town), 1942
Directed by Veit Harlan, starring Kristina Söderbaum. While Söderbaum was awarded the Volpi Cup for best actress at the Venice Film Festival, the film showcased German Agfacolor (as opposed to American Technicolour). The film earned the director the title of the

---

[101] Secret police report on the reception of *Feuertaufe*: Bundesarchiv Koblenz, R58/184, 08-10 Vol 145.1940, translated by Lutz Becker.

Third Reich's "pre-eminent colorist", according to recent historians.[102]

Hände am Werk
(Hands at Work – A Song of German Work), 1935
Filmed and edited by Walter Frentz.

Hans Westmar, 1933
Directed by Franz Wenzler, with music by Dr Ernst Hanfstaengel. Based on the life and death of National Socialist "martyr" Horst Wessel, whose main contribution was the eponymous song which became the battle anthem of the Nazi party. Hans Westmar, aka Horst Wessel, is murdered by Communists. The proletarian Communist idealist's clenched fist changes into a Nazi salute with his conversion. In October 1933 Goebbels initially banned the film claiming it did not do justice to Wessel, "whose heroic figure it belittles through inadequate representation, nor to the National Socialist movement, on which the state now rests."

Heideschulmeister Uwe Karsten (The Country Schoolmaster), 1933
Directed by Carl Heinz Wolff, starring Marianne Hoppe.

Das Herz der Königin (The Queen's Heart), 1940
Anti-imperialist historical film starring Zarah Leander, directed by Carl Froelich.

---

[102] *A New History of German Cinema*, edited by Jennifer M. Kapscynski & Michael D. Richardson (New York: Camden House, 2012, p.294.

Hitler's Kampf um Deutschland
(Hitler's Fight for Germany), 1932
Short documentary film.

Hitlerjunge Quex (Hitler Youth Quex), 1933
Directed by Hans Steinhoff the film contrasts heroic Nazi youth with the Communists rabble. Young Heini finds his life's purpose by joining the Hitler Youth, and is murdered by the enemy in pursuit of his patriotic duty. He dies murmuring Baldur von Schirach's Hitler Youth marching song, 'Our flag flutters before us…'

Ich klage an (I accuse), 1941
Directed by Wolfang Liebeneiner, the film portrayed a doctor who helps his wife who is suffering from multiple sclerosis, to die. "The film's purpose," wrote Liebeneiner in 1965, "was to test whether public opinion would approve of a law sanctioning death on demand within certain medical and legal safeguards. The test proved negative, the law was never passed, but the public debate on euthanasia which had been provoked immediately focused on the hitherto denied killing of mental patients and was instrumental in putting a stop to this… to this day I am convinced that the film has done good, perhaps even saved human lives." By 1st September 1941, however, 70,273 disabled people had already been "disinfected", in

other words gassed – and without being offered the choice.[103]

Immensee: Ein deutsches Volkslied (A German Folksong), 1943
Directed by Veit Harlan, starring Kristina Söderbaum, Carl Raddatz. After the great expense of *Die goldene Stadt*, Harlan proposed a money-saving option to Goebbels: to shoot three films – *Immensee, Opfergang* and another which was never completed - simultaneously using the same actors and sets. *Immensee* was one of the most successful and popular of all German films of the era. Harlan later wrote in his autobiography, "Of all the films that I made during the war, this was the only one which remained true to the original scenarios and was distributed just as I had foreseen."

Jud Süß, 1940
One of the most controversial films of the era, directed by Veit Harlan, starring Kristina Söderbaum, Ferdinand Marian, Heinrich George, Werner Krauß. According to historian Karlheinz Wendtland, "Probably the most famous Nazi propaganda film, the film's adaptation of Hitler's anti-Semitic agitation in *Mein Kampf*."[104] Another, Eric Rentschler, adds: "Jud Süß endures as a monstrous entity."

---

[103] Hans Schmid, "Es wird ein Signal, ein Weckruf sein!", *Telepolis* 02.01.2012, http://www.heise.de/tp/artikel/36/36066/1.html
[104] Karlheinz Wendtland, cited in Rentschler, *Ministry of Illusion*, p.150.

*Das junge Deutschland marschiert
(German Youth on the March)*, 1932
Short documentary film.

Kolberg, 1945
Directed by Veit Harlan, starring Kristina Söderbaum, Heinrich George, Paul Wegener.

Das Leben geht weiter (Life goes on), 1945
Directed by Wolfgang Liebeneiner, starring Marianne Hoppe and Heinrich George, with music by Norbert Schultze. Partially scripted by Joseph Goebbels. Filmed in Babelsberg and then Lüneburg (as the approaching armies made filming in Berlin untenable) between November 1944 and April 1945, it was the very last film of the Third Reich. As the British troops entered Lüneburg, Liebeneiner hid the film rushes in a church, and they have never been seen again.

Metropolis, 1927
Directed by Fritz Lang, written by Thea von Harbou. Starring Brigitte Helm, Gustav Fröhlich. Classic and influential silent film.

Münchhausen, 1943
Directed by Josef von Baky starring Hans Albers as the Baron. One of the earliest colour films and hugely expensive. For the harem scenes Von Baky made a detailed study of Alexander Korda's Arabian fantasy film,

The Thief of Bagdad, while the influence of Disney can also be clearly traced. The script was written by Erich Kästner, author of *Emil and the Detectives* and an opponent of the Nazi regime whose books had been burned and who had been interrogated several times by the Gestapo. He received a special exemption for the script and wrote under a pseudonym. It is said that the lackeys in the feast scenes were all members of the SS to ensure the safety of the props, which included real Meissen porcelain, gold and silver platters and chalices. Designed as pure escapism to distract the masses from the hardships of war, it remains an enjoyable and light-hearted film.

Die Nibelungen, 1924
Directed by Fritz Lang, written by Thea von Harbou. Both Goebbels and Hitler were fans, and later historians claimed that the film foreshadowed the rise of a Führer-type figure. Lang later claimed he hoped to counteract the pessimism of the Weimar period so that Germany could draw inspiration from its past.

Olympia, 1938
One of Leni Riefenstahl's astonishing masterpieces, deploying the athletes' performances to enhance the prestige and ideology of the Nazi regime, emphasising its supposed roots in classical antiquity.

Opfergang, 1944
Directed by Veit Harlan, starring Kristina Söderbaum, Carl Raddatz. It was shot (in colour) on alternate days with *Immensee* in order to save money. Distribution was held up for several months, though Goebbels admitted to the director that he often screened this sad but ultimately uplifting love story privately for his own enjoyment.

Quax, der Bruchpilot, 1941
A very successful film, directed by Kurt Hoffmann. Jolly little Heinz Rühmann stars as a coward who, to his dismay, wins a competition to learn to fly. Unsurprisingly, he wins through at the end.

Der Rebell, 1932
A favourite film of Goebbels, who praised it at his famous 1933 meeting with members of the film industry, Luis Trenker's film plays out against the background of the Tyrolean peasants' uprising against Napoleonic occupation.

Reise nach Tilsit, 1939
Directed by Veit Harlan, starring Kristina Söderbaum. Goebbels wrote in his diary on 11 October 1939: "A well-made, artistic film. But an excessively tormented, tragic view of marriage. Harlan is letting his own experiences show, and not even tastefully."

Die Reiter von Deutsch-Ostafrika
(The Riders of German East Africa), 1934
Directed by Herbert Selpin, the film depicts skirmishing between British and German forces in Africa. An unsubtle sub-text makes it clear that the colonies lost in the First World War will be re-conquered through German heroism.

Reitet für Deutschland (He rides for Germany), 1941
Directed by Arthur Maria Rabenalt. Banned after the war, and later re-issued with several anti-semitic scenes cut.

Romanze in Moll (Romance in a Minor Key), 1943
A tragic melodrama directed by Helmut Käutner, starring Marianne Hoppe, Paul Dahlke, Ferdinand Marian. Hoppe's character, torn between duty to her husband and love, commits suicide. Goebbels considered it defeatist and damaging to marriage and morale.

Rosen in Tirol, 1940
Light-hearted musical comedy directed by Géza von Bolváry.

Der Schritt vom Wege (Effi Briest), 1934
Directed by Gustaf Gründgens, based on the novel by Theodor Fontane, starring Marianne Hoppe once more torn between two men.

Der Spieler, 1938

Directed by Gerhard Lamprecht, starring Lida Baarova. Premiere on 1 September 1938; on 24 October happy family pictures of Goebbels with his children were published, and Baarova was summarily ejected from Germany. Her next German film - already shot, but pulled as Baarova became *persona non grata* - was only shown in 1950.

Stukas, 1941

Directed by Heinz Ritter, another morale-boosting film with a cheerful scene of singing pilots flying on their way to bomb Britain. By their blind obedience to the cause, they happily sacrifice the individual to the collective in honour of the Fatherland.

Triumph des Willens (Triumph of the Will), 1935

Directed by Leni Riefenstahl, under direct commission from Hitler, and against Goebbels' wishes.

Westwall, 1939

Forty-five minute documentary, directed by Fritz Hippler, about the building of the Siegfried Line.

Filmography of interviewees

This list includes only their main Nazi-era films, and a few other particularly notable pre- or post-war films.

Walter Frentz (1907-2004)
Joined the air force in 1938 and the SS in 1941, becoming Hitler's personal cameraman until the last days in the bunker, shooting mostly in colour from 1943.

1931: *Wildwasserparadiese in Österreich und Jugoslawien*, and two other kayaking films. Earliest handheld camerawork in a kayak!

1933: *Wasser hat Balken*, documentary filmed on board the ship *Hamburg* on the way to New York.

1933: *Sieg des Glaubens (The Victory of Faith)*, directed by Leni Riefenstahl. Frentz was recommended by Albert Speer.

1935: *Triumph des Willens (Triumph of the Will)* directed by Leni Riefenstahl.

1935: *Hände am Werk (Hands at Work – A Song of German Work)*, commissioned by the Propaganda Ministry.

1935: *Tag der Freiheit – Unsere Wehrmacht (Day of Freedom – Our Army)*.

1935-38: Documentaries, including *Farhtenbuch Albanien; Segelflieger auf der Wasserkuppe*.

1936: *Olympia,* directed by Leni Riefenstahl. Various sequences, eg. marathon runners.

Post-war: Cameraman on various travel, sport and nature documentary films.

Fritz Hippler (1909-2002)
Hippler joined the Nazi party at the age of seventeen, and became a member of the Sturmabteilung.
1933: Closely involved in Goebbels' book burning events.
1934: Wrote *Jugend fordert*, a book about Nazi youth.
1936: Worked on *Deutschen Wochenschau* newsreels.
1939-43: Head of Goebbels' film department (Reichsfilmdramaturg).
1940: *Feldzug in Polen (Polish Campaign)*. 40-minute documentary propaganda film.
1940: *Der Ewige Jud (The Wandering Jew)*, director. Considered one of the most racially offensive and effective propaganda films.
1943: Demoted due to drunkenness, worked as a cameraman on the front.
Post-war: Worked on documentary and corporate films, often using a pseudonym, and wrote several books.

Margot Hielscher (1919-)
Began work as a costume designer.
1940: *Das Herz der Königin (The Queen's Heart)*.
1941: *Auf Wiedersehn, Franziska*.
1942: *Ich sage ja (I say yes); Der Hochtourist*.
1943: *Fraue sind keine Engel (Women are no Angels)* - sang the title song, which became her signature song; *Liebespremiere (Love's Premiere); Reise in die Vergangenheit (Trip to the Past)*.
1944: *In flagrante; Der Täter ist unter uns (The culprit is amongst us)*.
1945: *Dreimal Komödie; Shiva und die Galgenblume* – the last film of the Third Reich, only finished in 1994!

1957, 1958: Represented West Germany twice at the Eurovision Song Contest, coming fourth in 1957 with *Telefon, Telefon*.
Post war: TV chat show, appeared in around 200 TV programmes, released many albums, won awards.

Lida Baarova (1914-2000)
1934: *Barcarole*.
1935: *Leutnant Bobby, der Teufelskerl* ; *Einer zuviel an Bord*.
1936: *Die Stunde der Versuchung; Verräter* ; *Svadlenka (The Seamstress)* in Czech.
1938: *Der Spieler; Preußische Liebesgeschichte* (first screened in 1950).
1953: *I Vitelloni*, directed by Federico Fellini.

Marianne Hoppe (1909-2002)
Married Gustaf Gründgens 1936; divorced 1946 when she became pregnant after an affair with Ralph Izzard, a British officer/Daily Mail foreign correspondent and possible cold war spy. Starred in many films, including:
1933: *Der Schimmelreiter, Heideschulmeister Uwe Karsten, Der Judas von Tirol*, as a patriotic wench to 'freedom fighter' Andreas Hofer.
1934: *Schwarzer Jäger Johanna*, her first title role, German patriotic resistance to Napoleon; *Krach um Jolanthe, Alles hört auf mein Kommando*.
1934/5: *Oberwachtmeister Schwenke*.
1935: *Die Werft zum grauen Hecht; Anschlag auf Schweda*.
1936: *Wenn der Hahn kräht; Eine Frau ohne Bedeutung*.
1936/7: *Der Herrscher*, directed by Veit Harlan.
1937: *Mein Sohn, der Herr Minister; Gabriele eins, zwei, drei; Kapriolen*, directed by Gustaf Gründgens.
1939: *Der Schritt vom Wege*, title role of Effi Briest.

1939: *Kongo-Express.*
1941: *Auf Wiedersehen, Franziska!* directed by Helmut Käutner. "Her performance here is magnificent... [the film] has nothing in common with other films of the period; it stands in lonely isolation as the work of an unhappy but superbly talented artist."[105]
1942: *Stimme des Herzens.*
1943: *Romanze in Moll.*
1943/4: *Ich brauche Dich.*
1944/5: *Das Leben geht weiter.*
Postwar: Continued as film, TV and theatre actor.
1990: Title role in *King Lear*, directed by Robert Wilson.

Gerhard Huttula (1902-1996)

Worked on advertising films in the 1920s before emigrating to Buenos Aires.
1937: Returned to Germany to support his mother, and joined Guido Seeber in the Ufa animated and special effects department.
1937: *Fern vom Land der Ahnen*, director of documentary.
1938: *Echo der Heimat*, director of documentary; *Spiel im Sommerwind*, special effects.
1939: *Der Geliebte* (all further films credits for special effects, unless otherwise stated); *Kongo-Expreß.*
1940: *Bal paré.*
1941: *Stukas; Friedemann Bach; Quax, der Bruchpilot.*
1942: *Hab' mich lieb! Die große Liebe; Andreas Schlüter; Dr Crippen an Bord; Diesel.*
1943: *Damals; Münchhausen; Der kleine Grenzverkehr.*
1944: *Opfergang; Die Frau meiner Träume; Große Freiheit Nr.7; Quax in Afrika.*

---

[105] David Stewart Hull, *Film in the Third Reich* (University of California Press, 1969) p.237.

1945: *Kolberg*, cameraman.
Postwar: Filmed a series of fairy tales and between 1958 and 1970 filmed over a thousand adverts.

Rudolf Klicks (1917-1997)
1932: *Tannenberg*
1934: *Die Reiter von Deutsch-Ostafrika (The Riders of German East Africa)*; *Liebe in St Moritz (The Champion of Pontresina)*; *Selbst ist der Mann; Der Flegel.*
1936: *Traumulus (The Dreamer).*
1938: Die vier Gesellen (The Four Companions) starring Ingrid Bergman.
1940s: Camera operator for *Die Deutsche Wochenschau.*

Brigitte Mira (1910-2005)
1930s: Esmerelda in *The Bartered Bride* (theatre).
1941: Kabarett der Komiker, Berlin.
1943: *Liese und Miese*, propaganda series. Mira played the 'bad' girl, who unwittingly gave useful information to the enemy, complained about rations, etc. Cancelled after ten episodes as Goebbels feared her character was becoming too popular.
Post war: Played important roles in many films directed by Rainer Werner Fassbinder, including *Fear Eats the Soul*, which won the International Critics' Prize at Cannes, 1975.

Theodor Nischwitz (1913-1994)
Apprenticeship at Ufa in Babelsberg, specialising in the trick film department.
1931: *F.P.1 Antwortet nicht (F.P.1 Doesn't Answer).*
1933: Ekstase (Ecstasy).
1933/4: Gold.

1934: Maskerade.
1935: *Amphitryon: Aus den Wolken kommt das Glück (Amphitryon: Luck comes from the Clouds).*
1938: *Im Zeichen des Vertrauens (Sign of Trust),*
1939: Worked on war reports.
1941: *Stukas.*
1942/3: *Besatzung Dora (Occupation Dora).*
1943: *Münchhausen.*
1943: War school in Potsdam.
1977: *The American Friend.*
1981: *Das Boot.*[106]

Arthur Maria Rabenalt (1905-1993)

1934: *Pappi*; *Was bin ich ohne Dich?; Eine Seibzehnjährige; Ein Kind, ein Hund, ein Vagabund (*banned, later re-released as *Vielleicht war's nur ein Traum*),
1935-1938: Worked in France, Italy and Austria after being accused of having Bolshevist tendencies.
1939: *Johannisfeuer (Midsummer Night's Fire).*
1940: *Weißer Flieder; Die drei Codonas; Achtung! Feind hört mit! (Attention! The enemy is listening!).*
1941: *Reitet für Deutschland (Riding for Germany); Leichte Muse.*
1942: *Fronttheater.*
1943: *Zirkus Renz; Liebespremiere.*
1944: *Am Abend nach der Oper.*

---

[106] http://www.deutsche-biographie.de/pnd138248052.html

Norbert Schultze (1911-2002)
Composer of film music and operas for children, including Struwwelpeter and Max und Moritz.
1938: Music for *Lili Marlene*, written in 1915 by Hans Leip, recorded by Lale Andersen in 1939 and became an international hit from 1941.
1939-1945 Many hit themes for films including *Von Finnland bis zum Schwarzen Meer; Bomben auf Engeland*; theme for *Feuertaufe*; theme for *Kolberg* and many more.

Kristina Söderbaum (1912-2001)
1936: *Onkel Bräsig.*
1938: *Jugend (Youth)*, directed by Veit Harlan. All her films from now on directed by Harlan. The first of many deaths by drowning for the "Reichs Water Corpse". *Verwehte Spuren (Covered Tracks).*
1939: Married Veit Harlan. *Das Unsterbliche Herz (The Immortal Heart); Die Reise nach Tilsit (Journey to Tilsit).*
1940: *Jud Süß*
1942: *Der große König; Die goldene Stadt.*
1943: *Immensee.*
1945: *Opfergang (The Great Sacrifice); Kolberg.*

Bibliography

Ascheid, Antje, *Hitler's Heroines: Stardom and Womanhood in Nazi Cinema* (Philadelphia: Temple University Press, 2003)
Barnouw, Erik, *Documentary: A History of the non-Fiction Film* (Oxford: Oxford University Press, 1983)
Berkholz, Stefan, *Goebbels' Waldhof am Bogensee. Vom Liebesnest zur DDR-Propagandastätte* (Berlin: Christoph Links Verlag, 2004)
Bruns, Jana Francesca, *Nazi Cinema's New Women* (Cambridge: Cambridge University Press, 2009)
Buchloh, Ingrid, *Veit Harlan: Goebbels' Starregisseur* (Paderborn: Ferdinand Schöningh, 2010)
Carter, Erica, *Dietrich's Ghosts: The Sublime and the Beautiful in Third Reich Film* (London: BFI, 2004)
Chambers II, Whiteclay; David Culbert, *World War II, Film, and History* (Oxford: Oxford University Press, 1997)
Cull, Nicholas John; David Holbrook Culbert; David Welch, *Propaganda and Mass Persuasion: A Historical Encyclopedia, 1500 to the present* (Santa Barbara: ABC-CLIO, 2003)
Fox, Jo, *Filming Women in the Third Reich (*Oxford & New York: Berg, 2000
Glesen, Rolf; J.P.Storm, *Animation under the Swastika: A History of Trickfilm in Nazi Germany, 1933-1945* (Jefferson: McFarland, 2012)
Hake, Sabine, *The Cinema's Third Machine: Writing on Film in Germany, 1907-1933* (University of Nebraska Press, 1993)
Hake, Sabine, *Popular Cinema of the Third Reich* (Austin: University of Texas Press, 2001)
Halle, Randall & Margaret McCarthy (eds.), *Light Motives: German Popular Film in Perspective* (Detroit: Wayne State University Press, 2003)
Veit Harlan, *Im Schatten meiner Filme* (Gütersloh: Sigbert Mohn Verlag, 1966)
Hitler, Adolf, *Mein Kampf*,
https://ia800302.us.archive.org/16/items/Mein_Kampf_Facsimilie/MK.pdf
Hoffmann, Hilmar, *The Triumph of Propaganda: Film and National Socialism, 1933-1945*, Vol. 1 (Providence, Oxford: Berghahn Books, 1996)

Hull, David Stewart, *Film in the Third Reich: A study of the German cinema, 1933-1945* (University of California Press, 1969)
Kapscynski, Jennifer M. & Michael D. Richardson (eds.), *A New History of German Cinema* (New York: Camden House, 2012)
Kershaw, Ian, *Popular Opinion and Political Dissent in the Third Reich: Bavaria 1933-1945* (Oxford University Press, 2002)
Knopp, Guido, *Hitler's Women* (New York: Routledge, 2001)
Koepnick, Lutz, *The Dark Mirror: German Cinema Between Hitler and Hollywood* (Berkeley: University of California Press, 2002)
Kreimeier, Klaus, *The Ufa Story: A History of Germany's Greatest Film Company, 1918-1945* (University of California Press, 1999)
Le Faucheur, Christelle Georgette, *Defining Nazi Film: The Film Press and the German Cinematic Project, 1933-1945* (Austin: PhD dissertation, University of Texas, 2012)
Leiser, Erwin, *"Deutschland, erwache!" Propaganda im Film des Dritten Reiches* (Reinbek: Rowohlt Verlag, 1968)
Leiser, Erwin, *Nazi Cinema* (London: Macmillan, 1974
Longerich, Peter, *Goebbels: A Biography* (London: Bodley Head, 2015)
Moeller, Felix, *The Film Minister: Goebbels and the Cinema in the Third Reich* (Stuttgart/London: Edition Alex Menges, 2000)
Munn, Michael, *Hitler and the Nazi Cult of Celebrity* (London: Robson Press, 2012)
O'Brien, Mary-Elizabeth, *Nazi Cinema as Enchantment: The Politics of Entertainment in the Third Reich* (Rochester NY: Camden House, 2004)
Rabenalt, Arthur Maria, *Film im Zwielicht: Uber den unpolitischen Film des Dritten Reiches und die Begrenzung des totalitären Anspruches* (Munich: Copress-Verlag, 1958)
Rees, Laurence, *Selling Politics* (London: BBC Books, 1992)
Rentschler, Eric, *The Ministry of Illusion: Nazi Cinema and Its Afterlife* (Cambridge: Harvard University Press, 1996)
Eric Rentschler, "Karsten Witte: The Passenger and the Critical Critic," *New German Critique*, no.74, special issue on Nazi cinema (spring/summer 1988) pp.15-22
Roepke, Andrea, Oliver Schroemm, *Stille Hilfe für braune Kameraden: Das geheime Netzwerk der Alt- und Neo-Nazis* (Berlin: Ch. Links Verlag, 2002)
Rosenbaum, Robert A., *Waking to Danger: Americans and Nazi Germany, 1933-41* (Santa Barbara: Praeger, 2010)
Salkeld, Audrey, *A Portrait of Leni Riefenstahl* (London: Random House, 1997)
Schultze, Norbert, *Mit dir, Lili Marleen. Die Lebenserinnerungen des Komponisten Norbert Schultze* (Zurich: Atlantis. 1995)

Sereny, Gitta, *Albert Speer: His Battle with Truth* (London: Picador 1996)

Söderbaum, Kristina, *Nichts bleibt immer so: Rückblenden auf ein Leben vor und hinter der Kamera* (Bayreuth: Hestia, 1984)

Tegel, Susan, *Nazis and the Cinema* (London: Hambledon Continuum, 2007)

vande Winkel, Roel, 'Nazi Germany's Fritz Hippler, 1909-2002,' *Historical Journal of Film, Radio and Television*, Vol 23, no.2 (2003)

von Oven, Wilfred, *Finale Furioso: Mit Goebbels bis zum Ende*, (Tübingen: Grabert-Verlag, 1974)

Weinberg, David, "Approaches to the Study of Film in the Third Reich: A Critical Appraisal," *Journal of Contemporary History*, vol.19, no.1 (Jan 1984) pp.105-126

Welch, David, *Propaganda and the German Cinema, 1933-1945* (London: I.B. Tauris, 2001)

Witte, Karsten, *Lachende Erben, Toller Tag. Filmkomödie im Dritten Reich* (Berlin: Verlag Vorwerk 8, 1995)

TV programmes

Joseph Goebbels, gesehen von der UFA-Star, Lida Baarova, film by Werner Koch and Günter Krause, WDR 1991.

Cinema Europe: The Other Hollywood, Photoplay Productions for BBC TV series on European silent cinema, written and directed by Kevin Brownlow and David Gill, 1995.

Sex and the Swastika, Twenty Twenty Television for Channel 4, produced and directed by Meredith Chambers, 1999.

Acknowledgements

With grateful thanks to Nikita Lalwani, Jeremy Levy, Roger Morsley Smith, Sarah Cruz, Hannah Winter-Levy and Sam Winter-Levy.

Aafa-Film AG, 82
Agfacolor, 14, 92, 122
Akademie der Künste, 32
Albers, Hans, 43, 44, 92, 126
Amphitryon, 57, 120, 136
Anna Karenina, 83
Argentina, 12, 20, 30, 42
Arnold, August, 50, 51
Arri camera, 51, 61
Augstein, Rudolf, 29
Aus den Wolken kommt das Glück, 120, 136

Baarova, Lida, 57, 58, 84, 105, 120, 130, 133, 140
Babelsberg, 17, 18, 23, 39, 40, 41, 42, 48, 54, 126, 135
Barcarole, 57, 120, 133
Battleship Potemkin, 81, 83
BBC, 1, 7, 11, 24, 30, 31, 39, 41, 139, 140
   The Nazis
      A Warning from History, 12
   Timewatch, 11
   We have ways of making you think, 11

Bechter, Edie, 102
Berchtesgaden, 12, 34, 65
Bild. See Bild Zeitung
Bild Zeitung, 68
Bismarck, 93, 120
Blaue Engel, 39, 82, 121
Bomben auf Engelland (Bombs on England). See Schultze, Norbert
Brandauer, Klaus Maria, 33
Brecht, Bertolt, 105
Brod, Max, 84
Bromberg, 25

Čapek, Karel, 84
Capriolen, 35, 121
Captains Courageous, 44
Cavalcanti, Alberto, 84

D. W. Griffiths, 85
DACHO, the Association of German Film Producers, 15
Daily Beast, 69
Daily Mail, 69, 70, 119, 133
Das Leben geht weiter, 126, 134
Deutsche Film AG (DEFA), 41
Deutsche Volksunion, 20

Dietrich, Marlene, 28, 39, 81, 121
Dreyfus, Carl, 35

Effi Briest, 33, 121, 129, 133
Eisenstein, Sergei, 81, 83
Es war eine rauschende Ballnacht, 57, 121
Ewige Jud, Der (*The Eternal Jew*), 62, 67, 121

Fassbinder, Werner, 53, 63, 135
Feld, Hans, 6, 15, 80, 83, 84
Feuertaufe, 93, 95, 96, 98, 122, 137
Filmbeobachtung (film observations), 17
Film-Kurier, 80, 81, 82, 84
Finale Furioso Mit Goebbels bis zum Ende. *See* von Oven, Wilfred
Frentz, Walter, 6, 13, 87, 123, 131
Frey, Gerhard, 20
Fröhlich, Gustav, 58, 120, 126

Garbo, Greta, 83
Garson, Greer, 37

Goebbels, Joseph, 1, 5, 6, 7, 8, 9, 12, 13, 14, 15, 16, 17, 18, 19, 20, 21, 22, 23, 24, 25, 27, 28, 29, 31, 33, 35, 36, 38, 41, 42, 43, 46, 49, 51, 53, 54, 55, 58, 59, 60, 61, 63, 65, 66, 68, 69, 70, 71, 73, 75, 77, 78, 83, 84, 86, 87, 91, 92, 93, 94, 95, 97, 99, 105, 106, 107, 108, 111, 112, 113, 117, 118, 119, 120, 123, 125, 126, 127, 128, 129, 130, 132, 135, 138, 139, 140
Goebbels, Magda, 15, 59, 60, 71, 73, 75, 77, 78, 105
Goldene Stadt, Die, 107, 108, 122, 125, 137
Göring, Hermann, 22, 32, 33, 35, 36, 38, 44, 95, 122
Grierson, John, 84
Gründgens, Gustaf, 32, 121, 129, 133

Hände am Werk, 87, 123, 131
Hans Westmar, 27, 123
Harlan, Veit, 38, 44, 45, 46, 59, 99, 100, 102, 103, 104, 105, 106, 107, 108,

109, 110, 111, 113, 114, 115, 117, 122, 125, 126, 128, 133, 137, 138
Heideschulmeister Uwe Karsten, 38, 123, 133
Helm, Brigitte, 40, 126
Herz der Königin, 54, 106, 123, 132
Hielscher, Margot, 5, 13, 53, 54, 55, 106, 119, 132
Himmler, Heinrich, 89, 110, 111
Hippler, Fritz, 6, 12, 62, 65, 67, 121, 130, 132, 140
Hitler, Adolf, 7, 8, 9, 12, 13, 14, 15, 16, 17, 18, 27, 33, 34, 35, 46, 60, 65, 66, 70, 73, 75, 77, 78, 79, 82, 86, 88, 89, 90, 94, 95, 97, 104, 105, 106, 118, 120, 124, 125, 127, 130, 131, 138, 139
Mein Kampf, 7
Hitler's Kampf um Deutschland, 8
Hitlerjunge Quex, 8, 28, 124
Hoppe, Marianne, 5, 13, 32, 34, 112, 121, 123, 126, 129, 133
Hotel Kaiserhof, 15, 49, 83
House of Rothschild, 65

Huttula, Gerhard, 5, 13, 39, 42, 46, 57, 134

Ich klage an, 93, 124
Immensee, 98, 116, 125, 128, 137
Irving, David, 90

Jaeger, Ernst, 82
Jews, 12, 15, 19, 22, 25, 26, 27, 28, 29, 30, 33, 34, 40, 41, 49, 53, 62, 65, 68, 69, 72, 75, 78, 80, 84, 102, 103, 104, 105, 109, 111, 112, 113, 114, 115, 120
Jolson, Al, 93
Jud Süß, 33, 45, 67, 72, 101, 102, 103, 108, 110, 112, 116, 125
Junge Deutschland marschiert, Das, 8, 126

Kaiserhof, Hotel, 84
Kästner, Erich, 5, 50, 127
Klicks, Rudolf, 5, 48, 135
Kolberg, 44, 45, 71, 93, 98, 99, 100, 102, 105, 116, 117, 118, 126, 135, 137
Körber, Hilde, 104, 105
Korda, Alexander, 43, 126
Kortner, Fritz, 104
Krauss, Werner, 111

Kritik, Die, 84

Lamarr, Hedy, 28
Lang, Fritz, 28, 39, 83, 126, 127
Lanke, 21, 22, 23, 24, 31, 58, 73, 95, 120
Leander, Zara, 29
Leben geht weiter, Das, 37
Liebeneiner, Wolfgang, 93, 113, 120, 126
Liese und Miese, 53, 135
Lili Marlene, 1, 93, 94, 137
Lorre, Peter, 28, 105
Löwenthal, Ewa, 72

Marian, Ferdinand, 111, 125, 129
Meisel, Edmund, 81
Meissner, Hans-Otto, 6, 12, 75, 79
Mephisto. *See* Gründgens, Gustaf
Metropolis, 39, 40, 126
Ministry of Public Enlightenment and Propaganda. *See* Propaganda Ministry
Mira, Brigitte, 5, 53, 135
Montagu, Ivor, 84
Mrs Miniver, 37
Müller, Renate, 34

Münchhausen, The Adventures of Baron M., 13, 40, 43, 44, 63, 92, 126, 134, 136

National Film Archive, Koblenz, 11
Negri, Pola, 29
Nibelungen, 83, 127
Nischwitz, Theodor, 5, 57, 61, 135
Nivea, 98

Oehm, Willy. *See* von Oven, Wilfred
Olympia, 34, 88, 127, 131
Operation Barbarossa, 95
Opfergang, 44, 45, 103, 106, 116, 125, 128, 134, 137
Ophuls, Max, 28
Oranienburg, 18, 26
Orphans of the Storm, 85

Pabst, G.W., 28
Pomsel, Brunhilde, 6, 13, 68, 69, 70
Pope Pius XII, 75, 79
Prinz, Rabbi Dr Joachim, 114
Propaganda
  in Mein Kampf, 7

Propaganda Ministry, 15, 17, 63, 68, 69, 70, 72, 87, 98

Quandt, Ello, 77
Quax, der Bruchpilot, 44, 128, 134

Rabenalt, Arthur Maria, 6, 12, 91, 110, 129, 136
Rebell, Der, 83, 128
Rees, Laurence, 11, 18, 24, 119
Reich's Ministry of Public Enlightenment and Propaganda. *See* Propaganda Ministry
Reichsfilmkammer (Reich's Film Chamber), 16
Reise nach Tilsit, 116, 128, 137
Reiter von Deutsch-Ostafrika, 48, 129, 135
Reitet für Deutschland, 91, 129, 136
Riefenstahl, Leni, 1, 6, 13, 34, 51, 52, 58, 78, 80, 81, 82, 84, 85, 86, 87, 88, 127, 130, 131, 139
Romanze in Moll, 33, 36, 129, 134
Rosen in Tirol, 97, 129

Rulf, Werner, 11

Sachsenhausen, 26, 34
Schloendorff, Volker, 18
Schultze, Norbert, 6, 13, 93, 122, 126, 137, 139
Schwanenwerder, 18, 58, 71, 120
Schwarzer Peter, 101
Sieg des Glaubens (The Victory of Faith), 87, 131
Singing Fool, 93
Siodmak, Robert, 28
Söderbaum, Kristina, 6, 13, 29, 44, 55, 99, 102, 103, 107, 113, 122, 125, 126, 128, 137
Späth, Hellmut, 34
Speer, Albert, 87, 131, 140
Spieler, Der, 60, 130, 133
SS (Schutzstaffel), 13
Stalingrad, 63, 71
Stukas, 63, 130, 134, 136

Thief of Baghdad, 43
Total War speech, 36, 71, 92, 99
Trenker, Luis, 83, 128
Triumph des Willens (Triumph of the Will), 34, 85, 87, 130, 131

Ufa, 39, 49, 83, 84, 93, 104, 113, 134, 135, 139

von Báky, Josef, 43
Von Finnland bis zum Schwarzen Meer, 95, 137
von Hindenburg, Paul, 75

von Oven, Wilfred, 5, 12, 19, 24, 29, 61, 73

Warsaw Ghetto, 65
Westwall, 62, 130
Wilder, Billy, 28
Wirsching, Otto Josef, 51
Wizard of Oz, 43